“There’s no way to be a perfect parent, and a million ways to be a good one.“

— Jill Churchill

For permission requests, contact:

Recognition Press
P.O. Box 3
Nashotah, Wisconsin
www.recognitionpress.com

Book cover and interior design by: command-s

First Edition: 2026
Published by Recognition Press – www.recognitionpress.com

Publisher's Cataloging-in-Publication Data

Smith, David A.
Knowing WHY Changed Everything: The Long-Awaited Owner's Manual for Ages 0-12 /David A. Smith. — First edition.

ISBN: 979-8-9997309-3-0 (paperback)
ISBN: 979-8-9997309-4-7 (ebook)

Subject headings: 1. Child development. 2. Parenting. 3. Child psychology. I. Title.

Published by Recognition Press, Nashotah, Wisconsin. 2026.

Printed in the United States of America
10 9 8 7 6 5 4 3 2 1

Knowing WHY Changed Everything

The Long-Awaited Owner's Manual *for* **Ages 0-12**

DAVID A. SMITH

Important Notice to Readers
This book is intended for informational and educational purposes only. It is not a substitute for professional medical, psychological, or therapeutic advice, diagnosis, or treatment.

This book does not provide medical or psychological advice.
The information presented here reflects the author's interpretation of developmental research and personal experience. While every effort has been made to ensure accuracy, the author and publisher make no representations or warranties about the completeness, reliability, or suitability of this information for any particular purpose.

Every child is unique.
Developmental timelines, behaviors, and needs vary significantly from child to child. What is described as "typical" in this book represents general patterns identified in research — not prescriptions for how your specific child should develop. Wide variation is normal and expected.

When to seek professional help:
If you have concerns about your child's development, behavior, or wellbeing, please consult with qualified professionals, including but not limited to:

- Your child's pediatrician or family physician
- Licensed child psychologists or psychiatrists
- Licensed clinical social workers or counselors
- Developmental specialists
- School counselors or educational psychologists

If you or your child are experiencing a mental health crisis, please contact:

- 988 — Suicide and Crisis Lifeline (call or text)
- Crisis Text Line — Text HOME to 741741
- Your local emergency services (911)
- Your nearest emergency room

The author is not a licensed medical or mental health professional.
The author's background includes decades of business experience, extensive study of human development and behavioral science, and personal experience as a parent. The perspectives shared in this book are informed by research but filtered through practical application. The author does not hold credentials in medicine, psychology, or child development as a clinical discipline.

Research evolves.
The developmental research referenced in this book represents current understanding as of the publication date. Scientific knowledge evolves, and recommendations may change as new research emerges. Readers are encouraged to stay informed and consult current sources.

Liability limitation:
The author and publisher specifically disclaim any liability, loss, or risk — personal, medical, psychological, financial, or otherwise — that is incurred as a consequence, directly or indirectly, of the use and application of any of the contents of this book.

A Note on the Research
Throughout this book, you will find references to developmental research, studies, and scientific findings. These references are intended to:

1. Ground the practical guidance in evidence rather than opinion
2. Provide readers with starting points for further exploration
3. Acknowledge the researchers whose work informs this material

The author has made every effort to accurately represent research findings. However, this book is a work of synthesis and interpretation for a general audience — not a peer-reviewed scientific publication. The "Research Behind These Words" sections at the end of each book provide an overview of key sources; they are not exhaustive literature reviews.

Readers seeking detailed methodology, statistical analysis, or comprehensive citations should consult the original research sources and peer-reviewed publications.

Acknowledgment
The guidance for this book is built on the work of countless researchers, clinicians, educators, and parents who have dedicated their careers to understanding child development. The author gratefully acknowledges this foundation.

By reading this book, you acknowledge that you have read and understood this disclaimer.

CONTENTS

INTRODUCTION

The Book I Wish Someone Had Given Me

I raised two daughters. As a single dad.

There were years I thought I was failing. Years I was sure something was wrong — with them, with me, with the whole endeavor of trying to turn small humans into functioning adults.

I read the books. I tried the techniques. I explained, negotiated, consequenced, and occasionally lost my mind in the cereal aisle of a grocery store while a three-year-old screamed about the wrong color spoon.

And through all of it, one question haunted me:
Why won't they just listen?

It took me decades to understand that I was asking the wrong question.

The Question That Changed Everything

The real question wasn't "why won't they listen?" It was: ***"What are they actually hearing when I speak?"***

Because here's what nobody told me — what I had to learn through years of study, observation, and yes, failure:

Children don't hear what we say. They hear what their developing brains can process.

And what their brains can process at two is radically different from four, which is radically different from seven, which is radically different from eleven. We speak to them as if they're small adults with full comprehension and limited cooperation. They're not. They're developing humans whose brains are under construction — literally, physically, neurologically under construction.

The toddler who "defies" you often doesn't understand your words the way you think they do. The five-year-old who "should know better by now" is running on cognitive architecture that can't yet do what you're asking. The ten-year-old who "doesn't care" is navigating a social and emotional landscape you can't see.

This isn't excuse-making. It's science. And understanding it changes everything.

That understanding — the neuroscience of what children actually hear when we speak — is what I explored in depth in *Why Won't You Listen? The Science of What Kids Really Hear When You Speak*. That book answers the "why" behind the communication gap: why your words don't land the way you intend, why their brains filter and translate and sometimes completely miss what you're saying, and why knowing this transforms how you communicate.

This book is the rest of the story.

Once you understand *why* the gap exists, you need to know what to expect at each stage — what your child's brain can actually do at two, at five, at seven, at eleven. You need a map of the terrain ahead. You need to know what's normal, what's concerning, and what they actually need from you at each developmental moment.

That's what this book provides.

If you've read *Why Won't You Listen?*, think of this as the companion field guide — the developmental roadmap that shows how those communication principles play out from birth to twelve. You'll recognize the concepts and see them unfold across every stage.

If you're starting here, you're in the right place. This book gives you the comprehensive picture of what's happening inside your child at each age — what their brain can do, what it can't yet, and what they need from you. It stands fully on its own.

That said, *Why Won't You Listen?* goes deeper into the neuroscience and gives you practical exercises you can use immediately — specific techniques for bridging the communication gap in real-time conversations. Many parents find that reading both gives them the full toolkit: the "why" behind the disconnect, the "what to expect" at each stage, and the "how" to communicate more effectively right now.

Start wherever makes sense for you. They work together, and they each work alone.

What This Book Is

This is an owner's manual.

Not a discipline guide. Not a collection of techniques to get compliance. Not a philosophy of parenting you need to adopt.

It's a guide to understanding what's actually happening inside your child at each stage of development — what their brain can do, what it can't do yet, and what that means for how you communicate, connect, and yes, sometimes just survive until bedtime.

The Foundation Years covers birth through age twelve — the years when the architecture of who they'll become is being built. Four developmental stages, each with its own logic, its own challenges, and its own gifts:

- **Before Words** (0-2) — When you are their entire world, and they're learning whether that world is safe
- **When Words Arrive** (2-5) — When language explodes but comprehension lags far behind
- **The Age of Reason** (5-7) — When logic emerges but remains partial and easily overwhelmed
- **The Forgotten Years** (7-12) — When everyone stops paying attention, but the real construction is happening

Each section stands alone. If you have a four-year-old, you can skip straight to "When Words Arrive." If you're in the thick of middle childhood, "The Forgotten Years" is waiting for you.

But there's value in reading the whole arc — in understanding where they've been, where they are, and where they're heading. Development is a story. This book tells it.

What This Book Isn't

This isn't a book that tells you exactly what to do in every situation. Children are too different, families are too varied, and anyone who promises a universal script is selling something.

This isn't a book that judges your choices. Whether you co-sleep or sleep train, breastfeed or bottle feed, use time-outs or don't — those decisions are yours. We're not here to weigh in.

This isn't a book that promises perfect children or perfect parents. "Good enough" is a research-backed concept — and it really is enough. Children don't need perfection. They need presence, consistency, and a parent willing to repair when things go wrong. That's the bar. And it's a worthy one.

And this isn't a book that blames. Not you, not your child, not your parents, not the culture. Blame doesn't help anyone. Understanding does.

What This Book Offers

Sight.

The ability to see your child clearly — not as a problem to solve or a behavior to correct, but as a developing human doing exactly what developing humans do.

Relief.

The realization that most of your struggles aren't failures. They're the predictable friction between what you expect and what's developmentally possible. That gap isn't your fault. It's the terrain.

Research.

Every claim in this book is grounded in developmental science. Not opinion. Not tradition. Not "because I said so." When we say "research shows," we mean it — and we provide the sources so you can verify for yourself.

Connection.

Because ultimately, that's what matters. Not compliance. Not performance. Connection. The relationship you build during these foundation years is the platform everything else stands on.

How to Use This Book

Read what you need, when you need it.

If you're in crisis with a three-year-old who won't stop hitting, go to "When Words Arrive" and read about what their brain can actually process right now. If you're wondering why your nine-year-old suddenly has opinions about everything and shares none of them with you, "The Forgotten Years" will help you see what's happening beneath the surface.

At the end of each section, you'll find a private reflection — questions for you, not about your child but about your own experience of that developmental stage. These aren't required. But many parents find that understanding what they carry from their own childhood changes how they parent now.

You'll also find a section called "The Research Behind These Words." This isn't filler. Every recommendation we make has research behind it. If someone challenges you, or if you want to learn more, the sources are there.

A Word Before We Begin

You're going to mess up.

I need you to hear that, because you probably already feel like you're messing up, and you need to know: you will. You'll lose your temper. You'll say the wrong thing. You'll miss cues and misread signals and handle something badly and lie awake at 2 AM wondering if you've broken your child forever.

You haven't.

The research is clear on this: children don't need perfect parents. They need good enough parents — parents who show up, who repair when things go wrong, who keep trying even when it's hard.

That's the standard. Good enough. Present. Willing to learn.

You're reading this book, which means you're already trying to understand.

Good enough is enough. The research is clear. You don't have to be perfect.

And — the fact that you're here, trying to understand? That's not just good enough. That's exactly the kind of parent your child needs.

So take a breath. Give yourself some grace. And let's look at what's actually happening inside that small, baffling, beautiful human you're trying to raise.

They're not giving you a hard time.

They're having a hard time.

And once you can see that clearly, everything changes.

— ***David A. Smith*** *Recognition Press*

BOOK ONE:

Before Words

A Field Guide for the First Two Years (0-2)

"The way we talk to our children becomes their inner voice."

— Peggy O'Mara

BOOK ONE CONTENTS

A Word Before You Begin

You're holding a tiny human who didn't come with instructions.

If you're like most new parents, you've already discovered this. You've Googled things at 2am that you never imagined Googling. You've second-guessed yourself fourteen times before breakfast. You've wondered — maybe out loud, maybe just in the quiet of your own exhaustion — am I doing this right?

Here's what nobody tells you: that question means you're already paying attention. And paying attention is most of the job.

This guide exists because parenting is one of the most important things humans do — and one of the least formally taught. We assume people will figure it out. We assume instinct will kick in. And sometimes it does. But instinct works best when it has something to work with. A framework. A few handholds. Some sense of what's actually happening inside that tiny, baffling, beautiful brain.

This is not a rulebook.

It's not a judgment of how you're doing, how you were raised, or how your mother-in-law thinks things should be done. It's not a collection of "shoulds" designed to make you feel guilty for every imperfect moment.

It's a field guide. A translation of what decades of research have revealed about infant brain development — written for real parents, in real life, with real limitations.

Some of what you read may surprise you. You might learn that things you thought didn't matter actually matter a lot. You might learn that things you've been stressing about matter less than you feared.

Some of what you read may be hard. If you didn't receive responsive, attuned care as a child yourself, reading about what babies need can surface grief for what you didn't get. That's normal. It's also an invitation — not to wallow, but to build something different. You can give what you didn't receive. It's harder, but it's possible. And it starts with knowing what to aim for.

You don't have to be perfect.

Researchers who study infant development talk about the "good enough" parent. Not the perfect parent — the good enough one. The one who gets it right about a third of the time, misses and repairs about a third of the time, and completely misses another third of the time. That's not failure. That's normal. That's human.

What matters isn't perfection. What matters is showing up. Repeatedly. Imperfectly. Responsively.

Your baby isn't grading you. They're learning — from your face, your voice, your touch, your presence — whether the world is safe, whether people can be trusted, whether their needs matter.

That's what this guide is about. Not the perfect parent. The present one.

Let's begin.

A Note on Cultures, Contexts, and How Families Differ

Parenting practices vary across cultures, communities, and families — and that's not a problem to be solved.

How babies are held, fed, soothed, and slept differs around the world, and many of those differences are adaptive, meaningful, and rooted in generations of wisdom. This guide does not presume to tell you which practices are "right."

The research cited here comes primarily from Western academic institutions, and we acknowledge that limitation. However, certain principles — responsiveness, attunement, consistent presence, repair after rupture — appear across cultures and throughout human history. How those principles are expressed varies. That they matter seems to be universal.

Where and how your baby sleeps, how you feed them, who holds them, how your extended family is involved — these are decisions shaped by your culture, your circumstances, your values, and your pediatrician's guidance. This guide offers principles, not prescriptions. You know your family. You know your baby. Take what serves you.

One more thing: if you're raising a child in a context different from how you were raised — whether by geography, culture, or choice — that's its own kind of challenge. You may be building without a blueprint, or actively building against a blueprint you don't want to repeat. Both are hard. Both are valid. Both are possible.

PART 1:

The Fourth Trimester (0-3 Months)

What's Actually Happening

Your baby just spent nine months in the most perfectly regulated environment imaginable — constant temperature, muffled sound, gentle motion, never hungry, never alone. And then, rather abruptly, they were evicted.

Welcome to the fourth trimester.

During these first three months, your baby is adjusting to... everything. Light. Sound. Air. Hunger. The bizarre sensation of being alone in space. Their nervous system is still developing the capacity to regulate itself. Their brain is building connections at a rate they'll never match again — roughly one million new neural connections per second.

And here's what the research tells us: those connections are being shaped by you.

During these early weeks, your baby's brain is "experience-dependent." That's a clinical way of saying: what happens to them literally shapes how their brain wires itself. Your face, your voice, your responsiveness — these aren't just comforting. They're construction materials.

What Your Baby Needs

YOUR FACE. Newborns can only see about 8-12 inches clearly — roughly the distance from your arms to your face. That's not an accident. Your face is their first curriculum. They study it. They learn from it. They're figuring out: What does love look like? What does safety look like? When I make a sound, what happens to that face?

YOUR VOICE. They've been hearing it for months, muffled through amniotic fluid. Now it's clear — and it's the most important sound in their world. Talk to them. Narrate your day. Tell them what you're doing while you change their diaper. It feels silly. Do it anyway. You're not teaching vocabulary yet; you're teaching connection.

YOUR RESPONSE. When they cry, they're not manipulating you. They're communicating the only way they know how. Research consistently shows that responding to their cries doesn't spoil them — it teaches them that their signals matter, that someone is listening, that the world is responsive. This is the foundation of trust.

When Do They Learn to Soothe Themselves?

This is the question behind the question. When someone tells you "don't pick them up every time, you'll spoil them," what they're really asking is: If you always soothe them, when will they learn to soothe themselves?

It's a fair question. And the answer is counterintuitive enough that it deserves its own space in this guide.

You don't teach a baby to self-soothe by withholding soothing. You teach them to self-soothe by soothing them so consistently that their brain internalizes the pattern.

Think of it like teaching someone to swim. You don't throw them into deep water and hope they figure it out. You hold them in the shallow end. You let their body learn what floating feels like while your arms are underneath them. And one day — not on your schedule, on theirs — they do it on their own. Not because you let go. Because they're ready.

Self-soothing works exactly the same way. Your consistent response is the shallow end. Your arms are teaching their nervous system what calm feels like. And their brain is taking notes — building the architecture that will eventually let them do it without you.

But that architecture develops on a timeline. Not yours. Theirs.

The Developmental Timeline

0–6 MONTHS: Your baby has zero capacity for self-soothing. None. The neural circuitry doesn't exist yet. Every calm-down must come from you — your arms, your voice, your heartbeat against theirs. This isn't a failure to develop independence. It's the biological reality of a nervous system that's still under construction. Expecting a three-month-old to soothe themselves is like expecting them to walk. The hardware isn't there.

6–12 MONTHS: Primitive self-soothing begins to emerge — thumb-sucking, rocking, clutching a comfort object. But these strategies only work if the child has a foundation of trust that someone will come when they really need it. The comfort object is a stand-in for you. It works because you were there first. A baby who has been consistently soothed develops the internal expectation of comfort — and can begin to access it in small doses on their own. A baby who hasn't doesn't develop that expectation. They don't self-soothe. They self-suppress. And those are very different things.

12–18 MONTHS: Growing capacity to tolerate brief frustration and brief separation. Brief. Not "cry it out for forty-five minutes." Brief means seconds becoming minutes, gradually, at the child's pace. And here's what the research shows clearly: this tolerance develops faster in children who were consistently responded to in the first year. Not slower — faster. Because their baseline state is calm, not anxious. They're stretching from a foundation of security, not reaching from a place of fear.

18–24 MONTHS: The beginning of real emotional vocabulary. With your help, they can start to name feelings. "You're frustrated" — said by you — starts to become "I'm frustrated" — said by them. That's self-regulation beginning. Not because you withheld comfort. Because you gave it so many times that they absorbed the language and the experience. They're doing for themselves what you did for them. That was always the goal.

The Research Is Clear

The most consistently soothed babies become the most independently regulated toddlers. This isn't theory. It's decades of attachment research, replicated across studies and across cultures. Secure attachment in infancy — built through responsive caregiving — predicts emotional independence later. Not dependency. Independence.

The "spoiling" myth gets it exactly backwards. It assumes that comfort creates weakness. The research shows that comfort creates security — and security is the platform from which independence launches.

So when someone tells you that picking up your crying baby will spoil them — when that voice comes from your mother-in-law, your neighbor, a well-meaning stranger, or the voice inside your own head that absorbed the message decades ago — you now have the answer:

They'll learn to handle it on their own. On their timeline. Because you taught them what calm feels like first. That's not spoiling. That's building.

A Note on the Self-Soothe vs. Self-Suppress Distinction

This matters enough to say plainly.

A baby who stops crying because they were soothed has learned: I was upset, someone came, I feel better. Their nervous system completed a cycle — distress, signal, response, relief. That completed cycle is what builds the pathway to self-regulation.

A baby who stops crying because nobody came has learned something different: I was upset, I signaled, nothing happened, I gave up. Their nervous system didn't complete the cycle. It abandoned it. The crying stopped — but not because they feel better. Because they stopped expecting to feel better.

From the outside, both babies are quiet. From the inside, they're in completely different places. One is calm. The other is resigned. One learned to regulate. The other learned that regulation isn't coming.

Over months and years, these two pathways produce very different children. The first child develops genuine emotional resilience — the ability to experience distress and move through it. The second child develops something that looks like resilience but isn't — the ability to shut down, disconnect, and appear fine while feeling anything but.

You can't always tell the difference by looking. But the child can tell. And their nervous system remembers.

Pick them up.

YOUR CALM. Here's something that might surprise you: research shows your baby can't regulate their own nervous system yet. They literally borrow yours. When you're calm, your calm helps regulate them. When you're chronically stressed, anxious, or dysregulated, they feel that too. This isn't about being perfectly zen — that's impossible with a newborn. It's about recognizing that your state affects their state, and giving yourself permission to seek support when you need it.

What It Looks Like When It's Working

- Baby cries; you respond; baby calms (not instantly — but eventually, with your help)
- Moments of eye contact where they seem to really see you

- Baby turns toward your voice
- Periods of alert, quiet attention — usually brief, but present
- You're exhausted but feel connected, not just depleted

What It Looks Like When Support Is Needed

- Baby seems inconsolable no matter what you try (this happens sometimes — it doesn't mean you're failing, but talk to your pediatrician if it's persistent)
- You feel disconnected, numb, or resentful toward your baby (this can be a sign of postpartum depression or anxiety — please reach out for help)
- You're so depleted you can't respond, or you're responding with frustration more often than not (you need support, not judgment)

Simple Connection Builders (0-3 Months)

SKIN-TO-SKIN CONTACT. Hold your baby against your bare chest. Research shows this regulates their temperature, heart rate, and stress hormones — and yours too.

FACE-TO-FACE TIME. When they're in a quiet, alert state (brief windows — catch them when you can), just look at each other. Make expressions. Let them study you.

MIRROR THEIR EXPRESSIONS. If they open their mouth, open yours. If they raise their eyebrows, raise yours back. This is the first "conversation" — and it's building their social brain.

NARRATE YOUR WORLD. "Now I'm picking you up. Now we're going to the kitchen. That's the refrigerator. It's very exciting, I know." Silly? Yes. Effective? Also yes.

HOLD THEM DURING FEEDS — even if bottle-feeding. The feeding position — close, cradled, face-to-face — isn't just about nutrition. It's about connection.

A Word for the Exhausted Parent

You're not sleeping. You're not showering regularly. You may have eaten cereal for three meals yesterday. You're operating on a level of exhaustion you didn't know was possible, and someone keeps telling you to "enjoy every moment."

Here's permission to not enjoy every moment.

Some moments are just survival. Some moments you're counting the minutes until someone else can hold the baby. Some moments you wonder what you've gotten yourself into.

That's normal. That's not failure. That's the reality of the fourth trimester.

What matters isn't enjoying every moment. What matters is showing up — even exhausted, even imperfect, even when you're not sure you're doing it right.

You're doing it right enough. You're here. You're trying.

That counts.

PART 2:

The Awakening (3-6 Months)

What's Actually Happening

Something shifts around three months. The fog begins to lift — for both of you.

Your baby is waking up to the world. Their vision sharpens. Their neck strengthens. They start to discover that those strange things floating past their face are their hands — and that's the most fascinating development in human history, as far as they're concerned.

More importantly for our purposes: they're becoming social in a whole new way.

During these months, your baby transitions from mostly receiving care to actively participating in exchanges. They smile with intention now — not just gas. They vocalize and then pause, waiting for you to respond. They're learning the rhythm of conversation long before they have words.

This is "serve and return" in action. They serve (a coo, a look, a wiggle). You return (a smile, a word, a touch). They serve again. Back and forth. It looks like playing. It's actually architecture.

Harvard's Center on the Developing Child calls these exchanges "the building blocks of brain development." Every time you respond to your baby's bid for connection, you're reinforcing neural pathways that say: My signals matter. The world responds. I can affect what happens to me.

This is the root system of everything that comes later — language, emotional regulation, relationships, even their sense of self. You're not just entertaining them. You're wiring them.

What Your Baby Needs

RESPONSIVENESS, NOT PERFECTION. You won't catch every coo. You won't return every serve. That's fine. Research suggests you need to be "in sync" with your baby about 30% of the time for healthy development. Thirty percent! That leaves a lot of room for missed cues, diaper emergencies, and moments when you're just trying to drink your coffee while it's still warm.

What matters is the pattern: they reach out, you respond, connection happens. Repeatedly. Imperfectly. Consistently enough.

RECIPROCAL EXCHANGES. This is the age to lean into back-and-forth "conversations." When they make a sound, make one back. When they look at something, look at it with them and name it. When they smile, smile back and say something. You're teaching them the fundamental structure of human communication: I act, you respond, we're connected.

This, by the way, is the foundation for everything in *Why Won't You Listen?* — the idea that communication isn't just about transmitting information, it's about connection. Your baby is learning that now, before they have a single word.

YOUR NARRATION. Keep talking to them. Describe what you're doing. Describe what they're doing. "You're kicking your legs! Those are some fast legs. Are you going somewhere? I don't think you can walk yet, but I admire the ambition."

This feels ridiculous. It's also incredibly valuable. You're not teaching them vocabulary (that comes later). You're teaching them that voices carry meaning, that language is connected to experience, that words and life go together.

FACIAL EXPRESSIONS AND TONE. Your baby is becoming a sophisticated reader of faces and voices. Research shows they can tell the difference between happy, sad, and angry expressions. They respond to the music of your voice — the rise and fall, the warmth or tension — even when they can't understand the words.

This is why *how* you talk to your baby matters as much as *that* you talk to them. They're not processing content yet. They're processing emotion. They're learning: What does love sound like?

What It Looks Like When It's Working

- Genuine back-and-forth exchanges — coo, respond, coo, respond
- Social smiles that light up when they see you
- Baby "talks" to you with sounds and expressions, then pauses expectantly
- Longer periods of alert, engaged interaction
- You find yourself having "conversations" that feel almost real (because they are)

What It Looks Like When Support Is Needed

- Baby rarely makes eye contact or seems to look through you
- Limited response to your face or voice
- You consistently feel disconnected or are struggling to engage
- Baby seems either constantly distressed or unusually passive

These can be signs of various things — some developmental, some relational, some temporary. If you're concerned, talk to your pediatrician. Early support makes a significant difference.

Simple Connection Builders (3-6 Months)

THE PAUSE. When your baby vocalizes, respond — then wait. Give them space to "answer" back. This turn-taking teaches the rhythm of conversation.

PEEK-A-BOO (EARLY VERSION). Cover your face briefly, then reveal it with a smile. You're teaching object permanence (you still exist even when hidden) and building anticipation — their brain is starting to predict what comes next.

MIRROR GAMES. Make exaggerated expressions and watch them try to imitate. Stick out your tongue. Open your mouth wide. Raise your eyebrows. They're not just mimicking — they're learning that faces communicate, that expressions mean something, that we can share states with each other.

TUMMY TIME CONVERSATIONS. While they're working on those neck muscles, get down on their level. Face-to-face on the floor. Talk to them. Make it a connection moment, not just physical exercise.

READING ALOUD. They don't understand the words. They don't care about the plot. They care about your voice, the rhythm, the closeness, the ritual. Board books with high-contrast images are great, but honestly? Read them the newspaper if you want. It's your voice they're after.

SING. Badly. Repeatedly. The same song forty-seven times in a row. Babies love repetition — it's how their brains learn patterns. And they don't know you can't carry a tune. You're their favorite performer regardless.

A Word for the Exhausted Parent

By now you've probably heard "it gets easier" enough times to want to throw something at the next person who says it.

Here's the truth: it doesn't get easier exactly. It gets different. The sleepless newborn phase gives way to new challenges — teething, mobility, separation anxiety, opinions about everything. Parenting is just a series of phases, each with its own particular flavor of exhaustion.

But something else is happening too. Those moments of connection — the smile that's clearly meant for you, the way they calm in your arms, the "conversations" that feel genuinely reciprocal — these start to add up. The relationship is becoming real. You're not just keeping a small human alive anymore. You're building something together.

On the hard days, that might not feel like enough. That's okay. Some days you're just surviving. But on the days when you catch a glimpse of who this little person is becoming, and you realize you're part of that becoming?

That's the good stuff. That's what you're building toward.

PART 3:

The Explorer (6-12 Months)

What's Actually Happening

Everything starts moving.

Somewhere in these months, your baby discovers locomotion — rolling becomes scooting becomes crawling becomes cruising becomes (for some early movers) walking. The world that was once limited to what you brought to them is now available for direct investigation.

This changes everything.

Developmentally, your baby is in the grip of two competing drives: the urge to explore and the need for security. They want to crawl toward the fascinating electrical outlet. They also want to know you're right there, watching, ready to help if needed.

Watch a baby this age in a new environment: they'll venture out, then look back at you. Venture a little further, look back again. That look back is called "social referencing" — they're checking your face to see if the situation is safe. Research shows your expression literally guides their behavior. If you look calm and encouraging, they'll keep exploring. If you look anxious or alarmed, they'll retreat.

You are their home base. Their secure foundation. The place from which they explore and to which they return.

This is attachment in action — not as a feeling, but as a system. They're learning: I can go out into the world because I have somewhere safe to come back to. I can take risks because someone is watching out for me.

This is also when separation anxiety typically emerges. Your baby now understands that you're a specific, irreplaceable person — and that you can leave. This is actually a cognitive achievement (they understand object permanence now), but it doesn't feel like an achievement when they're screaming because you went to the bathroom.

What Your Baby Needs

A SECURE BASE. Be present. Be watchable. Be the place they look back to. When they check in with a glance, meet their eyes. When they bring you a toy (the first "sharing"), receive it with enthusiasm. When they crawl back to your lap after an expedition, welcome them.

ENCOURAGEMENT TO EXPLORE. Your job isn't to prevent all risk — it's to provide safe enough conditions for them to take appropriate risks. Let them struggle a little with a toy before helping. Let them navigate small challenges. Resist the urge to constantly intervene. Their confidence grows from mastering things themselves, with you nearby but not doing it for them.

YOUR CALM DURING THEIR STORMS. Emotional regulation is still a work in progress. Way in progress. When they get frustrated — and they will, constantly, because they want to do things their bodies can't do yet — they need your help to calm down. Not distraction (though that works sometimes). Not dismissal ("you're fine"). Actual co-regulation: your calm presence helping their nervous system settle.

This is the early training ground for everything that comes later. Research suggests that every time you help them regulate now, you're building their capacity to regulate themselves later. This is what *Why Won't You Listen?* addresses from the language side — children need to borrow our regulation before they can own their own.

PREDICTABLE ROUTINES. Babies this age are building mental models of how the world works. When things happen in predictable patterns — meals, naps, baths, bedtime rituals — they develop a sense of order and safety. They can't tell time, but they can recognize sequences. And knowing what comes next reduces anxiety.

WORDS, WORDS, WORDS. They're not talking yet, but they're absorbing language at an astonishing rate. Research shows that by the time they say their first word, they'll already understand dozens. Keep narrating. Keep naming things. Keep describing what's happening. You're filling a reservoir they'll draw from soon.

A Word About "No"

Your baby is mobile now. They're reaching for everything, crawling toward everything, putting everything in their mouth. And you're saying "no" constantly. Maybe dozens of times a day.

It works. They reach for the cord, you say "no," they pull back. You think: *Good. They learned.*

They didn't.

This is one of the most important and most misunderstood moments in the first two years, so let's slow down and look at what actually happened inside your baby's brain when your "no" worked.

What They Can't Do Yet

Your baby cannot connect the word "no" to the concept "that object is dangerous." That's an abstraction — a link between a sound, a category of risk, and a future consequence — that requires cognitive architecture their brain hasn't built yet. They won't be able to make that connection reliably for years.

So if they didn't learn that the cord is dangerous, what did they learn?

What They Actually Learned

If your "no" was calm, they learned a trained response: that particular sound means stop what I'm doing. Not why. Not what's dangerous. Just: that sound means stop. It's the same mechanism as a dog responding to a command — a conditioned association between a sound and an action, with no understanding underneath it.

This is why they'll reach for the same cord tomorrow. And the next day. And the day after that. They're not being defiant. The lesson you think you taught didn't actually transfer. You stopped the moment. You didn't build the understanding. That's not a failure on their part — it's a limitation of what their brain can do right now.

If your "no" was sharp, loud, or frequent, they may have learned something more consequential. Not that the cord is dangerous — but that reaching for things makes you upset. That exploring their world produces a negative response from the person they depend on most.

Repeat that lesson enough and something shifts. Not overnight. Gradually. The baby who was reaching for everything — which is exactly what a healthy, curious, developing brain is supposed to do — starts reaching less. They start checking your face before they touch anything. They start hesitating where they used to explore.

From the outside, this looks like learning. It looks like a well-behaved child. You might even get compliments: *"Your baby is so good."*

Underneath, something different is happening. The drive to explore — which is the engine of every cognitive, motor, and social development leap in these years — is being suppressed. Not because the child decided exploring isn't worthwhile. Because the cost of exploring became too high. The price was your displeasure, and that's a price no baby can afford to pay.

Why This Matters Beyond This Moment

Curiosity at this age isn't a personality trait. It's a developmental necessity. When your baby reaches for something, they're not misbehaving. They're doing their job — investigating the world, building neural connections, developing the cause-and-effect reasoning that everything else depends on. *What happens when I pull this? What does this feel like? What does that person do when I touch this?*

Every one of those experiments, when allowed to happen safely, builds brain architecture. Every one of those experiments, when consistently shut down, represents a pathway that didn't get built.

This doesn't mean you never say "no." Safety is non-negotiable. You're going to stop them from pulling the lamp off the table. You're going to keep them away from the stove. That's your job.

But there's a difference between stopping a dangerous behavior and building a habit of suppression. The difference is in the ratio — how often "no" is the tool you reach for — and in what comes after.

What to Do Instead

REDIRECT INSTEAD OF REJECT. When they reach for the cord, move their hand and offer something they can reach for. "Not that one — here, try this." You've stopped the behavior without stopping the exploration. The message isn't *don't reach*. The message is *reach for this instead.*

REMOVE THE HAZARD, NOT THE CHILD. Baby-proofing isn't laziness. It's strategy. Every dangerous object you move out of reach is a "no" you don't have to say. And every "no" you don't have to say is an exploration that gets to happen.

NARRATE INSTEAD OF COMMAND. Instead of "no" when they touch something new, try narrating: "That's the plant. It has dirt. Dirt is messy. Feel the leaf — that's soft." You're turning a potential "no" into a language lesson, a sensory experience, and a moment of shared attention. This is the "serve and return" from earlier in this guide — they explored (serve), you responded with engagement (return), and their brain just got a rep it wouldn't have gotten if the interaction had stopped at "no."

SAVE "NO" FOR WHEN IT MATTERS. If "no" is used for everything — the cord, the dog's tail, the remote, the couch cushion, the shoe, the leaf — it becomes noise. It loses whatever power it had. But if "no" is rare — reserved for genuine danger, delivered with calm urgency — it actually means something. Their brain registers it as different from the usual flow. Scarcity gives it weight.

The Bigger Picture

Here's what the research tells us, and what you'll see play out across every chapter of this book: the children who develop the strongest initiative, the most resilient problem-solving, the most confident exploration of their world — are not the children who were told "no" least. They're the children whose curiosity was protected while they were kept safe.

Those two things — protecting curiosity and ensuring safety — feel like they're in conflict. They're not. They're the same job, approached from two directions. You're keeping them safe *so they can keep exploring*. Not keeping them safe *by stopping the exploration*.

It's the difference between a guardrail and a wall. A guardrail lets them see the view. A wall blocks it entirely. Both prevent falling. Only one preserves what they came to the edge for.

Your baby is standing at the edge of their world, reaching for everything in it. That's not a problem to manage. That's development in action. Your job is to build the guardrail — and then let them look.

A Note for Parents Who Heard "No" Too Often

If you grew up in a home where "no" was the default — where curiosity was treated as inconvenience, where exploration was met with sharp correction, where you learned early to stop reaching — this section may have been hard to read.

You might recognize yourself in the description of the child who checks the parent's face before touching anything. You might remember the feeling of wanting to investigate something and deciding it wasn't worth the risk.

You might also notice that "no" comes out of your mouth faster and louder than you intend. Not because you chose it. Because it was installed.

Here's what matters: you're reading this. You're recognizing the pattern. That recognition is the first step in changing it. You don't have to do it perfectly. You just have to catch yourself more often than you miss — and when you miss, repair. Move toward the redirect. Move toward narrating. Move toward the guardrail instead of the wall.

Every time you protect their curiosity instead of suppressing it, you're writing different code. For them. And for yourself.

What It Looks Like When It's Working

- Baby explores confidently but checks back with you regularly
- Clear attachment behaviors — wanting you specifically when upset, showing preference for familiar caregivers
- Moments of frustration followed by (eventual) calming with your help
- Growing ability to play independently for short stretches while you're nearby
- First "words" appearing (mama, dada, or approximations) — sounds tied to meaning
- Joy at reunions after separations

What It Looks Like When Support Is Needed

- Baby doesn't seem to notice or care when you leave or return
- Extreme distress that doesn't calm with your comfort

- No babbling or attempts at communication by 9 months
- Limited interest in exploring or interacting with objects
- Persistent difficulty with transitions or new situations

Again — these can have many explanations. Some babies are temperamentally more cautious. Some are processing faster internally than they show externally. Every child's timeline is different. But if you're concerned, early evaluation is always worthwhile.

Simple Connection Builders (6-12 Months)

FOLLOW THEIR LEAD. When they're interested in something, get interested with them. Joint attention — looking at the same thing together, sharing focus — is a crucial developmental skill. "Oh, you found a leaf! Look at that leaf. It's green. It's crunchy. Leaves are very interesting."

NAME EMOTIONS. Start building their emotional vocabulary before they can speak. "You seem frustrated. That toy isn't doing what you want. That's annoying, isn't it?" You're teaching them that feelings have names, that feelings are normal, that someone understands.

This is straight from *Why Won't You Listen?* territory — the idea that children need language for their emotional experience before they can communicate it effectively.

PEEK-A-BOO (ADVANCED). Now they get it. Now they anticipate. Now they laugh before you even reveal your face. Play it constantly. You're building prediction, memory, and the delightful knowledge that things (and people) that disappear come back.

CONTAINER PLAY. Putting things in and taking them out. Dropping things and watching them fall. Handing you things so you can hand them back. These aren't just games — they're experiments in cause and effect, in how the world works, in how relationships work (I give, you give, we exchange).

PAT-A-CAKE AND SIMPLE SONGS WITH MOTIONS. Repetitive songs with actions teach sequencing, prediction, and imitation. They also create rituals — shared moments that belong to just the two of you.

READING WITH INTERACTION. Now they can point. They can turn (and chew) pages. They can respond when you ask "where's the dog?" Make reading interactive. Let them participate. It's not about getting through the book — it's about the back-and-forth.

A Word for the Exhausted Parent

This age is relentless. They're mobile but have no judgment. They're curious about everything, especially the dangerous things. They need constant supervision and they're not great conversationalists yet. You may feel like a combination security guard and entertainment director, with neither position offering adequate compensation.

Here's the thing: you're also watching a person emerge.

Those first intentional communications — the pointing, the showing, the primitive words — are them reaching out to share their experience with you. Not just needing you. Wanting you to see what they see. That's profound. That's the beginning of real relationship.

And that game you've played four hundred times that they still find hilarious? That's not tedium (okay, it's a little tedium). It's trust. They know what to expect. They can predict the joy. You are a reliable source of delight in an unpredictable world.

That matters more than you know.

Before We Continue

A truth that often goes unspoken

Before we enter the toddler years — before we talk about tantrums and "no" and the relentless testing of limits — there's something foundational we need to address.

It's something that's often overlooked in parenting books. Something that might be uncomfortable to read. But it may be the most important thing in this entire guide.

You Are Their Weather

Your baby doesn't just notice your emotional state. They absorb it.

This isn't metaphor. Research shows that infants are exquisitely attuned to caregiver affect from the earliest weeks of life. They read your face, your voice, your muscle tension, your breathing. And their nervous system responds — not by thinking about it, but automatically, below conscious awareness.

When you're calm, your calm helps them regulate. When you're chronically stressed, anxious, or angry, they feel that too — and their developing stress-response system adjusts accordingly.

You are the weather they live in.

What the Research Shows

Studies on infant cortisol — the primary stress hormone — show that babies' stress levels correlate with their caregivers'. When mothers exhibit elevated cortisol, infants do too. When mothers receive interventions that reduce their stress, infant cortisol levels also decrease.

The Still Face research demonstrates that infants as young as three months are deeply affected by caregiver emotional unavailability. Even brief periods of maternal unresponsiveness produce measurable distress. Extended or chronic unavailability — emotional or physical — can disrupt healthy development.

Babies are not passive recipients of care. They're active participants in a regulatory system that depends on caregiver attunement. They can't calm themselves yet. They borrow your nervous system to do it.

This is co-regulation — and it's not optional. It's how human development works.

What This Means (and Doesn't Mean)

It does not mean you have to be perfectly calm.

That's impossible, especially with a baby or toddler. You will be tired. You will be frustrated. You will have moments of anger, anxiety, despair. That's not failure. That's parenthood.

What matters isn't the absence of negative emotion. What matters is:

- The overall climate, not every individual storm
- Repair after rupture
- Your capacity to return to calm (eventually)
- Your awareness that your state affects theirs

It does mean your emotional regulation matters more than you might think.

Not for your sake (though that too). For theirs. Every time you calm yourself in the midst of chaos, you're teaching their nervous system that calm is possible. Every time you stay regulated during their dysregulation, you're showing them that big feelings are survivable.

You're not just managing your own stress. You're modeling regulation for a brain that's still learning how it's done.

The Anger Question

Let's talk about anger specifically, because this is where parents often feel the most guilt and confusion.

Babies and toddlers can be infuriating. The sleep deprivation, the relentlessness, the irrationality, the mess — it's genuinely maddening sometimes. Feeling anger doesn't make you a bad parent. It makes you human.

But expressing anger at your baby or toddler — yelling, harsh tone, aggressive movements — registers in their nervous system as threat. They can't understand that you're frustrated about the situation. They just feel the intensity directed at them. And their system responds with fear.

Occasional ruptures aren't catastrophic. You'll lose your temper sometimes. Everyone does. What matters is:

- You recognize it
- You repair it (calming yourself, then reconnecting)
- It's not the dominant pattern

If you find yourself frequently angry, regularly yelling, or unable to control your reactions — that's a signal. Not that you're a bad person, but that you need support. More help with the baby. More sleep. Therapy. Medication. Something. Because research shows that chronic anger in the home environment shapes developing brains in ways that last.

Practical Implications

TAKE CARE OF YOURSELF. Not as a luxury. As a parenting strategy. Your regulation is their regulation. Sleep, support, breaks, whatever you need to stay closer to okay — it's not selfish. It's foundational.

TAG OUT WHEN YOU CAN. If you have a partner, family, or friend who can take over when you're at your limit — use them. Walking away when you're about to lose it isn't abandonment. It's wisdom.

REPAIR MATTERS. When you do lose it — when you yell or shut down or aren't the parent you want to be — repair. Come back. Reconnect. Say (even to a baby who doesn't understand the words), "Mommy got really frustrated. That was scary. I'm here now. We're okay." They understand the tone, the touch, the return of connection.

MONITOR THE CLIMATE. Step back periodically and ask: What's the emotional weather in our home? Is it mostly warm with occasional storms? Or is it chronically tense, unpredictable, stormy? If it's the latter, something needs to change — and that something is almost always support for the adults.

WATCH FOR CHRONIC STRESS SIGNALS IN YOURSELF. Persistent irritability. Feeling disconnected from your baby. Going through the motions without joy. Intrusive thoughts. Rage that scares you. These aren't character flaws. They're symptoms. Postpartum depression and anxiety are real, treatable, and more common than most people admit. Get help.

When It's More Than Exhaustion: A Word on Postpartum Mental Health

There's tired, and then there's *something else.*

Every new parent is exhausted. Every new parent has moments of doubt, frustration, even regret. That's normal. That's the job.

But sometimes what you're experiencing isn't just the hard parts of parenting. Sometimes it's your brain chemistry responding to one of the most significant biological and psychological events a human can go through.

Postpartum depression and anxiety are common. Not rare. Not a sign of weakness. Not something that only happens to "other people." Research suggests that 1 in 5 mothers and 1 in 10 fathers experience significant postpartum mental health challenges. The numbers may actually be higher — many cases go unreported because parents feel ashamed or assume they're just "not handling it well."

What it might look like:

- Persistent sadness, emptiness, or hopelessness that doesn't lift
- Anxiety that feels constant, not just occasional worry
- Difficulty bonding with your baby, or feeling detached, numb, or going through the motions
- Intrusive thoughts that frighten you — thoughts of harm coming to yourself or your baby
- Rage that feels disproportionate or out of your control
- Inability to sleep even when the baby is sleeping, or wanting to sleep all the time
- Feeling like you've made a terrible mistake, or that your baby would be better off without you
- Physical symptoms: racing heart, chest tightness, inability to eat, panic attacks

Here's what you need to know:

These symptoms are not your fault. They're not a reflection of your love for your baby. They're not a moral failing. They're a medical condition, and they're treatable.

You would not feel ashamed of getting treatment for a broken bone. This is no different.

What helps:

- **Tell someone.** Your partner, a friend, your doctor, a therapist — anyone you trust. Silence makes it worse. Saying it out loud often brings relief.

- **Talk to your healthcare provider.** Postpartum depression and anxiety respond well to treatment — therapy, medication, or both. You don't have to white-knuckle through this.

- **Postpartum Support International** (postpartum.net) offers a helpline, online support groups, and resources in multiple languages. Their helpline is **1-833-943-5746 (1-833-9-HELP4MOMS)** — free, 24/7, confidential, available in multiple languages.
- **If you're having thoughts of harming yourself or your baby**, call **988** (Suicide and Crisis Lifeline) or go to your nearest emergency room. This is a medical emergency, and help is available.

One more thing:

Getting help isn't taking something away from your baby. It's giving them the parent they need. A parent who gets treatment is a parent who can show up. A parent who suffers in silence is depleted, disconnected, and running on empty.

Your baby needs you regulated more than they need you perfect. If your nervous system is in crisis, getting help *is* the parenting.

You're not broken. You're not failing. You might just need support that you haven't asked for yet.

Please ask.

Word for Parents Who Grew Up in Stormy Weather

If your childhood home was characterized by unpredictable anger, chronic tension, or emotional volatility — you know what it's like to live in bad weather.

You might have worked hard to create something different. And you might find, to your distress, that under pressure you sound exactly like the parent you swore you'd never become.

This is not destiny. But it is momentum. The patterns we absorbed in childhood are strong, and they emerge most when we're depleted.

Be compassionate with yourself when it happens. And be honest about what you need. Sometimes breaking cycles requires more than willpower. It requires help — therapy, support groups, parenting programs, whatever resources can give you new tools and help you process old wounds.

Your children will benefit from the weather you create. And so will you.

PART 4

The Threshold (12-24 Months)

What's Actually Happening

Words arrive.

Not all at once, and not on schedule (the range of "normal" is enormous — don't compare your child to your neighbor's). But somewhere in this year, your baby becomes a toddler, and your toddler becomes a talker. Single words become two-word combinations. Pointing and grunting becomes "more milk" and "no sleep" and the ever-popular "MINE."

This is exhilarating. This is also... a lot.

Because here's what else is happening: your toddler is developing a sense of self. They're realizing they're a separate person with separate desires — and those desires frequently conflict with yours. They want the thing they can't have. They want to do the thing themselves, even when they can't. They want autonomy while simultaneously being terrified of it.

Welcome to the toddler paradox.

Developmentally, this is crucial work. They're individuating — becoming their own person, separate from you. This requires them to push against you, to test limits, to assert preferences, to have (many, many) opinions. It's not defiance. It's development.

But here's where *Why Won't You Listen?* becomes directly relevant: they're also developing language faster than they're developing emotional regulation. They can say more than they can manage. They have words for wants but not yet for feelings. They can demand but not yet negotiate.

And critically — their brain is processing language differently than yours. The research in *Why Won't You Listen?* shows that children hear and interpret language through developmental filters that adults have long since forgotten. What you think you're communicating and what they're receiving may be very different things.

This is the year to remember: **connection before direction**. You can't instruct a child who doesn't feel connected to you. You can't reason with a brain in the middle of an emotional flood. The relationship is the vehicle for everything else.

What Your Baby Needs

LANGUAGE, LANGUAGE, LANGUAGE — BUT MATCHED TO THEIR LEVEL. Talk to them constantly, but simply. Short sentences. Concrete words. One instruction at a time. Their processing speed isn't yours. Give them time to understand and respond.

EMOTIONAL CO-REGULATION (STILL, ALWAYS). Their feelings are huge and their capacity to manage them is tiny. Tantrums aren't manipulation — they're overflow. Their system is overwhelmed and they need your help to come back down. Stay calm (or fake it). Get low. Offer presence. Words can come after the storm passes.

AUTONOMY WITHIN LIMITS. They need to feel powerful. Give them choices, but bounded ones. "Do you want the red cup or the blue cup?" lets them feel in control without you negotiating whether cups are required. Pick your battles. Let them win the ones that don't matter.

PREDICTABILITY AND ROUTINE. Even more important now. Toddlers are control enthusiasts living in a world where they control almost nothing. Routines give them something to rely on, something to predict. Transitions are hard because they represent loss of control. Warning helps: "In five minutes we're going to put on shoes."

CONNECTION BEFORE CORRECTION. When you need to redirect, set a limit, or address behavior — connect first. Get on their level. Make eye contact. Touch them gently if they're receptive. *Then* give the instruction. A connected child is a cooperative child. A disconnected child is a defended child.

This is the core principle of *Why Won't You Listen?*: children can't hear you when their nervous system is in defense mode. They can't process instruction when they feel disconnected or threatened. The relationship isn't separate from the communication — it *is* the communication.

YOUR PRESENCE DURING THEIR BIG FEELINGS. Don't send them away to calm down alone. Stay close (even if they're pushing you away). Let them know the feeling is survivable and the relationship is intact. "You're really mad. I'm here. I'll help you."

What It Looks Like When It's Working

- Language exploding — new words appearing constantly
- Able to follow simple instructions (when they want to)
- Shows range of emotions and recovers from upsets (with help)
- Plays alongside other children, even if not fully with them
- Tests limits but responds to reconnection
- Shows affection, empathy, humor
- Tantrums happen but don't last forever

What It Looks Like When Support Is Needed

- Few or no words by 18 months
- Doesn't respond to their name or simple instructions
- No interest in other people or children
- Extreme or prolonged tantrums that don't respond to any intervention
- Sudden regression in skills they'd already developed

Trust your instincts. If something feels off, ask. Early intervention services exist for a reason, and earlier is always better than later.

The Gap: What They Can Do vs. What They Understand

Here's what developmental research tells us that will save you enormous frustration if you can internalize it early:

Your child's performance vastly exceeds their comprehension.

They can say words they don't fully understand. They can follow simple instructions without grasping the *why* behind them. They can repeat rules while being completely incapable of following those rules. They can nod when you explain something and have processed almost none of it.

This isn't defiance. This isn't manipulation. This is development.

The Mismatch in Action

Watch a 20-month-old who's been told "hot — don't touch" reach for the stove anyway. They can say "hot." They might even say "no touch." But the connection between the word, the concept, the consequence, and their own impulse to reach? That neural pathway isn't built yet.

Watch a 2-year-old who's been told "we're leaving in five minutes" melt down when it's time to go. They heard the words. They might have even repeated them back. But they have no concept of time, no ability to prepare emotionally for transitions, no capacity to connect "five minutes" to the future moment when leaving actually happens.

Watch a toddler hit another child right after being told "no hitting." They know the rule. They can recite the rule. But impulse control — the ability to stop an action between the urge and the behavior — is one of the last things to develop. It requires prefrontal cortex maturation that won't be complete for decades.

They're not ignoring you. They're not testing you (well, sometimes they are — but not the way you think). They literally cannot do what you're expecting.

Why This Matters

When parents mistake performance for understanding, they expect too much. And when children fail to meet impossible expectations, parents get frustrated. That frustration often leads to discipline — consequences for behavior the child couldn't actually control.

This is where research shows damage can happen. Not from occasional frustration (that's human), but from chronic mismatch:

Child can't do what parent expects

Parent interprets this as defiance

Parent punishes or withdraws

Child feels confused, unsafe, disconnected

Parent feels ineffective, angry, guilty

Connection erodes

Behavior gets worse (because behavior is communication, and they're communicating that something is wrong)

Cycle repeats

The research in *Why Won't You Listen?* addresses this mismatch in detail — how children process language differently than adults, how their brains filter and translate what they hear, how much gets lost between your mouth and their understanding.

But it starts here, in these early years, with this fundamental gap between what they can perform and what they actually know.

What This Means for You

LOWER YOUR EXPECTATIONS FOR COMPREHENSION. Way lower. Assume they understand about half of what you think they understand. Then cut that in half again for anything involving time, consequences, or abstract concepts.

REPEAT WITHOUT FRUSTRATION. You will say the same thing hundreds of times. This isn't because they're not listening. It's because learning requires repetition, and some things can't be learned until the brain is ready.

WATCH FOR THE PERFORMANCE TRAP. Just because they can say it doesn't mean they get it. Just because they did it yesterday doesn't mean they can do it today. Just because they know the rule doesn't mean they can follow it.

DISCIPLINE DEVELOPMENTALLY. Research suggests a 1-year-old needs redirection, not consequences. An 18-month-old needs you to stop the behavior and offer an alternative, not an explanation of why it's wrong. A 2-year-old might be ready for very simple, immediate consequences — but lectures, time-outs, and "think about what you did" are meaningless. They can't think about what they did. Not the way you mean.

CONNECT BEFORE YOU CORRECT. This is always the answer. When they've done something wrong, the first move is connection, not discipline. Get on their level. Make contact. Regulate together. *Then* address the behavior — simply, briefly, without expecting them to understand the way you do.

REMEMBER: THEY'RE NOT GIVING YOU A HARD TIME. THEY'RE HAVING A HARD TIME. The behavior that looks like defiance is almost always overwhelm, developmental limitation, or unmet need. Respond to what's underneath, not just what's on the surface.

A Note for Parents Who Were Expected to Know Too Much Too Soon

If you grew up with parents who expected adult-level understanding and compliance from you as a child — if you were punished for things you couldn't control, if "you should know better" was a constant refrain — this section might be painful to read.

You might recognize the pattern. You might feel grief for the child you were. You might feel the pull to repeat what was done to you, even as you consciously want something different.

That pull is strong. Under stress, we default to what was modeled for us.

When you feel yourself expecting too much, getting frustrated at what looks like defiance, wanting to punish — pause. Take a breath. Ask yourself: Is this a developmental limitation or actual defiance? Nine times out of ten, with a child under three, it's developmental.

You can break the pattern. It takes awareness, intention, and practice. You won't do it perfectly. But every time you respond to developmental limitation with patience instead of punishment, you're writing new code — for yourself and for your child.

Simple Connection Builders (12-24 Months)

SPECIAL TIME. Even ten minutes a day of one-on-one, child-led play makes a difference. Let them direct. Follow their lead. Don't teach. Don't correct. Just be with them in whatever they're doing. This fills their connection tank and makes everything else easier.

NAME FEELINGS CONSTANTLY. "You're frustrated because the blocks fell down." "You're excited to go outside!" "You're sad because Daddy left." You're building their emotional vocabulary — the words they'll eventually use to express themselves instead of screaming.

GIVE WORDS FOR WHAT THEY WANT. When they're reaching and grunting, supply the word. "You want the ball? Ball. Can you say ball?" Don't withhold the thing to force the word — that creates frustration, not learning. Give the word and the thing together.

SIMPLE CHOICES. "Which book?" "This shirt or that shirt?" "Banana or apple?" Choices build autonomy without chaos.

ROUGHHOUSE PLAY. Physical play — tickling, chasing, wrestling gently — builds connection, releases tension, and teaches regulation (how to get excited and then calm down). Follow their cues. Stop when they say stop.

RITUALS AND REPETITION. The same song before bed. The same game after bath. The same book seventeen times in a row. Rituals build security. Repetition builds competence. Let them anticipate, predict, participate.

CONNECT DURING TRANSITIONS. Before you leave, during pickup, at bedtime — these transition moments are rich opportunities. Give a special goodbye ritual. Have a reunion routine. Mark the moments when connection might feel threatened.

A Word for the Exhausted Parent

Toddlers are wonderful and toddlers are terrible, often within the same five-minute window. They are discovering independence in the most dependent possible way. They are learning to talk by saying "no" constantly. They are building self-regulation by falling apart regularly.

It is exhausting.

Here's what might help: this too is a phase. Not in the dismissive "enjoy every moment" way — but in the genuine "this particular flavor of hard will evolve into a different flavor of hard" way.

And here's what's also true: you are laying foundations that will last decades. The way you respond when they're melting down. The way you stay calm when they can't. The way you hold the limit while holding the relationship. The way you give them words for their inner experience.

They won't remember these moments specifically. But their nervous system will. Their sense of safety will. Their capacity for relationship will.

You're not just surviving toddlerhood. You're building the brain and heart of a future adult.

No pressure.

(Okay, some pressure. But you've got this. Probably. Most of the time. And that's enough.)

PART 5

Building What You Can't See

A Closing Word

Two years.

Seven hundred and thirty days of feeding, holding, soothing, changing, waking, watching, worrying, wondering. Days that felt endless and months that somehow vanished. A blur of firsts — first smile, first laugh, first word, first step, first tantrum, first "no," first "mama," first time they ran toward you with arms open.

And through all of it, something was being built that you couldn't see.

Not just a bigger body, though that too. Not just new skills, though those are obvious. Something deeper. Something that won't show up on a growth chart or a developmental checklist.

You were building architecture.

Neural pathways that will shape how they process emotion for the rest of their life. Attachment patterns that will influence every significant relationship they ever have. A nervous system calibrated to expect — or not expect — that the world will respond when they reach out.

You were teaching them, before they had words, whether people can be trusted. Whether their needs matter. Whether connection is safe. Whether they are worthy of love.

That's what these two years were about. Not the sleep schedules (though those matter). Not the milestones (though those are exciting). Not whether you did everything "right" (you didn't — no one does).

What mattered was showing up. Responding. Repairing when you missed. Staying present through the hard parts. Being the safe place they could venture out from and return to.

The Research Is Clear

Children who receive consistent, responsive care in the first two years develop brains that are wired for connection, regulation, and resilience. They're more likely to form secure attachments. They're better able to manage stress. They have stronger foundations for language, learning, and relationships.

But here's what's equally important: this isn't about perfection. It's about "good enough." It's about patterns, not individual moments. It's about repair being as valuable as getting it right the first time.

You didn't have to be perfect. You just had to keep showing up.

What Comes Next

The toddler years transition into the preschool years. Language explodes. Imagination ignites. Social worlds expand. New challenges emerge — sharing, waiting, managing disappointment, navigating friendships, understanding rules.

But the foundation you've built doesn't disappear. It becomes the platform everything else is built on.

The child who learned in infancy that their cries would be answered becomes the preschooler who can ask for help with words — the very journey that *Why Won't You Listen?* explores. The toddler who experienced co-regulation during meltdowns becomes the child who's developing self-regulation. The baby who was given words for feelings becomes the child who can say "I'm frustrated" instead of hitting.

You won't see direct lines. Development is messy and non-linear. But the work you did in these first two years? It's in there. It's wired in. It's part of who they're becoming.

A Word About Your Own History

If you came to parenthood without a good map — if your own childhood was marked by absence, inconsistency, chaos, or pain — these two years may have been doubly hard.

You were building something for your child that you never received yourself. You were running a program you had to write from scratch, without examples to draw from. You were giving what you didn't get, and sometimes that required giving what you didn't even know existed.

That's exhausting. And it's also remarkable.

Breaking cycles is harder than continuing them. Building new patterns takes more energy than defaulting to old ones. If you've been doing this work — parenting intentionally, not just instinctively — you've been doing something profound.

It may not feel profound. It may feel like just surviving. But your child is receiving something you didn't. And that changes trajectories. Not just for them, but for their children someday. And their children's children.

Research shows that improved parenting in one generation can positively influence up to three subsequent generations. You're not just raising a child. You're redirecting a river.

The Manual You Were Never Given

This guide was an attempt to give you something most parents never receive: a translation of what research knows about infant development, written for real life.

It wasn't complete. No guide could be. It didn't address every situation, every temperament, every cultural context. It offered principles, not prescriptions. And it probably told you some things you already knew intuitively and some things that surprised you.

If it helped you understand what was happening inside your baby's brain — if it gave you permission to be imperfect — if it reminded you that what you're doing matters even when it doesn't feel like it — then it did what it was meant to do.

The rest is up to you.

You've got this. Probably. Most of the time.

And that's enough.

The Mirror: Your Private Reflection

For your eyes only.

Parenting is shaped by what we experienced as children — for better or worse. Sometimes we're repeating patterns we loved. Sometimes we're running from patterns we hated. Often we're doing both simultaneously, without quite realizing it.

These questions aren't about judgment. They're about awareness. Because you can't change patterns you don't recognize.

Take a few minutes. Answer honestly. No one needs to see this but you.

About Your Own Childhood:

1. When you were upset as a young child, how did your caregivers typically respond?
    - Comfort and presence
    - Dismissal ("You're fine")
    - Frustration or anger
    - Absence or distraction
    - I don't remember

2. How was affection expressed in your home growing up?
    - Freely and frequently
    - Occasionally, when earned
    - Rarely or never
    - Inconsistently — warm sometimes, cold others
3. When you think about your early childhood, the predominant feeling is:
    - Safety and warmth
    - Loneliness
    - Anxiety or unpredictability
    - Numbness or blankness
    - A mixture I'm still sorting out
4. What do you wish your parents had done differently in your first years?
5. What do you want to repeat from your own childhood?

About Your Parenting Now:

6. When your baby cries, your first internal reaction is usually:
    - Concern — what do they need?
    - Tenderness — I want to help
    - Frustration — what now?
    - Anxiety — am I doing this wrong?
    - Numbness — I'm too tired to feel anything
7. What's the hardest part of parenting an infant/toddler for you?
8. When do you feel most connected to your child?
9. When do you feel most disconnected?

10. Is there a pattern from your own childhood that you notice yourself repeating, even when you don't want to?
11. What's one thing you're doing well that you want to keep doing?
12. What's one thing you want to do differently going forward?

Looking Forward:

13. What kind of relationship do you hope to have with your child when they're older?
14. What do you want them to remember about these early years?
15. What support do you need — but haven't asked for?

A Note on These Reflections

If answering these questions surfaced difficult feelings — grief for what you didn't receive, guilt about patterns you're repeating, anxiety about whether you're doing enough — that's normal. It's also information.

Parenting has a way of excavating our own childhood, whether we want it to or not. The small human in front of you is a mirror, reflecting back not just who you are but who you were, and who raised you.

If your own history is making it harder to be the parent you want to be, consider talking to someone. A therapist who specializes in attachment or perinatal mental health can help you process the past while building something new.

You can give what you didn't receive. It's harder. It's possible. And it's one of the most important things a person can do.

A Note on Cultures, Contexts, and How Families Differ

(Expanded from earlier)

Parenting practices vary across cultures, communities, families, and generations — and that variation is not a problem to be solved.

How babies are held, fed, soothed, and slept differs around the world and across time. Extended family involvement, physical closeness practices, feeding approaches, sleep arrangements, who provides primary care — all of these vary, and many variations are adaptive, meaningful, and rooted in wisdom that predates any research study.

This guide does not presume to tell you which practices are "right."

What the research suggests is universal:

- Babies need responsive, consistent care from at least one committed caregiver
- Secure attachment forms through repeated cycles of need, response, and repair

- Co-regulation — borrowing a caregiver's calm — is how babies learn to self-regulate
- Serve and return interactions build neural pathways for communication and connection
- The quality of early relationships shapes brain development in lasting ways

What varies — and should:

- Who provides that care (parents, grandparents, extended family, community)
- Specific practices around sleep, feeding, holding, and soothing
- How emotion is expressed and responded to
- Cultural values around independence vs. interdependence
- The role of community in raising children

The research cited in this guide comes primarily from Western academic institutions, and we acknowledge that limitation. Studies conducted in one cultural context don't automatically apply to all others. However, the core principles of responsiveness, attunement, and consistent presence appear across human societies and throughout human history.

This guide offers principles, not prescriptions.

You know your family. You know your culture. You know your baby. You know what resources and support you have access to, and what constraints you're operating within. Take what's useful here. Adapt what needs adapting. Leave what doesn't fit.

The goal isn't to parent like a research study. The goal is to raise a human who knows they're loved, who trusts that the world will respond when they reach out, and who has a foundation strong enough to build a life on.

How you get there is yours to figure out.

The Research Behind These Words

For clinicians, educators, researchers and those who want to verify the claims: full citations for claims made in each section follow. This book is designed to be recommended to clients and families as an accessible entry point to developmental research.

On early brain development and experience: Research documents that the brain develops most rapidly in the first three years of life, with early experiences directly shaping neural architecture (Center on the Developing Child at Harvard University, "The Science of Early Childhood Development," National Scientific Council on the Developing Child, 2007). The brain is described as "experience-dependent," meaning it develops in response to environmental input, particularly the quality of caregiver-infant interactions (Shonkoff, J.P. & Phillips, D.A., eds., From Neurons to Neighborhoods: The Science of Early Childhood Development, National Academy Press, 2000). Neural connections form at a rate of approximately one million per second during the first years of life (Center on the Developing Child at Harvard University, "Brain Architecture," developingchild.harvard.edu).

On serve and return interactions: "Serve and return" interactions — reciprocal exchanges between infant and caregiver — have been identified as foundational to healthy brain development (Center on the Developing Child at Harvard University, "Serve and Return," developingchild.harvard.edu). Research shows these back-and-forth interactions build neural connections essential for communication, social skills, and emotional regulation (Greenspan, S.I. & Shanker, S.G., *The First Idea: How Symbols, Language, and Intelligence Evolved from Our Primate Ancestors to Modern Humans*, Da Capo Press, 2004).

On attachment theory: Attachment theory, foundational to understanding infant-caregiver relationships, was developed through decades of research (Bowlby, J., *Attachment and Loss, Vol. 1: Attachment*, Basic Books, 1969). The classification of attachment styles — secure, anxious-avoidant, anxious-resistant, and disorganized — emerged from systematic observation research (Ainsworth, M.D.S., Blehar, M.C., Waters, E., & Wall, S., *Patterns of Attachment: A Psychological Study of the Strange Situation*, Erlbaum, 1978).

On attachment and brain structure: Research found that variations in maternal sensitivity were associated with differences in infant brain volumes, including subcortical grey matter (Sethna, V., et al., "Maternal Sensitivity and Infant Brain Volumes," *Brain Structure and Function*, 222(5), 2017). Studies using the Strange Situation Procedure have linked attachment security in infancy to brain structure differences observable years later (Moutsiana, C., et al., "Insecure Attachment During Infancy Predicts Greater Amygdala Volumes in Early Adulthood," *Journal of Child Psychology and Psychiatry*, 55(10), 2014).

On the Still Face Experiment: The Still Face Paradigm demonstrated that infants as young as three months are highly sensitive to caregiver responsiveness (Tronick, E., Als, H., Adamson, L., Wise, S., & Brazelton, T.B., "The Infant's Response to Entrapment Between Contradictory Messages in Face-to-Face Interaction," *Journal of the American Academy of Child Psychiatry*, 17(1), 1978). When caregivers become unresponsive, infants show predictable patterns of distress, withdrawal, and dysregulation — evidence of their early social expectations and need for connection (Tronick, E.Z., "Emotions and Emotional Communication in Infants," *American Psychologist*, 44(2), 1989).

On co-regulation and stress response: Research on the hypothalamic-pituitary-adrenal (HPA) axis documents that infants cannot regulate their own stress responses and rely on caregivers for co-regulation (Gunnar, M.R. & Donzella, B., "Social Regulation of the Cortisol Levels in Early Human Development," *Psychoneuroendocrinology*, 27(1-2), 2002). Studies show that maternal sensitivity affects infant cortisol levels and long-term stress response patterns (Albers, E.M., Riksen-Walraven, J.M., Sweep, F.C., & de Weerth, C., "Maternal Behavior Predicts Infant Cortisol Recovery from a Mild Everyday Stressor," *Journal of Child Psychology and Psychiatry*, 49(1), 2008).

On the "good enough" parent: The concept originated with pediatrician and psychoanalyst D.W. Winnicott (Winnicott, D.W., "Transitional Objects and Transitional Phenomena," *International Journal of Psycho-Analysis*, 34, 1953; Winnicott, D.W., *The Child, the Family, and the Outside World*, Penguin, 1964). Contemporary research supports the finding that perfect attunement isn't necessary — or even desirable. Studies suggest that being "in sync" with an infant approximately 30% of the time supports healthy development, with repair after misattunement being as valuable as initial attunement (Tronick, E.Z. & Gianino, A., "Interactive Mismatch and Repair: Challenges to the Coping Infant," *Zero to Three*, 6(3), 1986).

On intergenerational transmission: Research documents that parenting patterns transmit across generations, with both positive and negative patterns showing continuity

(Van IJzendoorn, M.H., "Intergenerational Transmission of Parenting: A Review of Studies in Nonclinical Populations," *Developmental Review*, 12(1), 1992). Studies show that improved parenting skills in one generation can positively influence subsequent generations (Chen, Z.Y. & Kaplan, H.B., "Intergenerational Transmission of Constructive Parenting," *Journal of Marriage and Family*, 63(1), 2001).

On language development and early interaction: Research shows that the quantity and quality of language exposure in the first years predicts later language abilities (Hart, B. & Risley, T.R., *Meaningful Differences in the Everyday Experience of Young American Children*, Brookes Publishing, 1995). However, conversational turns — back-and-forth exchanges — matter more than sheer volume of words heard, supporting the importance of responsive, interactive communication (Romeo, R.R., et al., "Beyond the 30-Million-Word Gap: Children's Conversational Exposure Is Associated With Language-Related Brain Function," *Psychological Science*, 29(5), 2018).

On skin-to-skin contact: Research demonstrates that skin-to-skin contact (kangaroo care) regulates infant temperature, heart rate, breathing, and stress hormones (Feldman, R., Eidelman, A.I., Sirota, L., & Weller, A., "Comparison of Skin-to-Skin (Kangaroo) and Traditional Care: Parenting Outcomes and Preterm Infant Development," *Pediatrics*, 110(1), 2002). Benefits extend to full-term infants and include improved breastfeeding, reduced crying, and enhanced bonding (Moore, E.R., Bergman, N., Anderson, G.C., & Medley, N., "Early Skin-to-Skin Contact for Mothers and Their Healthy Newborn Infants," *Cochrane Database of Systematic Reviews*, 11, 2016).

On infant sleep: Research acknowledges significant cultural and individual variation in infant sleep practices, with no single arrangement proven optimal for all families (McKenna, J.J. & McDade, T., "Why Babies Should Never Sleep Alone: A Review of the Co-Sleeping Controversy in Relation to SIDS, Bedsharing and Breast Feeding," *Paediatric Respiratory Reviews*, 6(2), 2005). Studies emphasize safe sleep practices while recognizing that responsive nighttime parenting supports attachment (Ball, H.L., "Breastfeeding, Bed-Sharing, and Infant Sleep," *Birth*, 30(3), 2003).

On infant feeding: Research supports breastfeeding benefits while acknowledging that responsive bottle-feeding also supports secure attachment (Britton, J.R., Britton, H.L., & Gronwaldt, V., "Breastfeeding, Sensitivity, and Attachment," *Pediatrics*, 118(5), 2006). Studies emphasize that the feeding relationship — warmth, responsiveness, and attunement during feeding — matters for attachment regardless of feeding method (Ainsworth, M.D.S. & Bell, S.M., "Some Contemporary Patterns of Mother-Infant Interaction in the Feeding Situation," in *Stimulation in Early Infancy*, Academic Press, 1969).

On postpartum mental health: Research documents that postpartum depression and anxiety affect 10-20% of new mothers and can impact infant development through reduced responsiveness and attunement (Field, T., "Postpartum Depression Effects on Early Interactions, Parenting, and Safety Practices: A Review," *Infant Behavior and Development*, 33(1), 2010). Studies show that treatment of maternal depression improves outcomes for both mothers and infants, emphasizing the importance of screening and support (Forman, D.R., et al., “Effective Treatment for Postpartum Depression Is Not Sufficient to Improve the Developing Mother-Child Relationship,” *Development and Psychopathology*, 19(2), 2007).

On the neuroscience of crying response: Research shows that infant cries activate specific neural circuits in caregivers, preparing them for responsive action (Swain, J.E., et al., "Brain Basis of Early Parent-Infant Interactions: Psychology, Physiology, and In Vivo Functional Neuroimaging Studies," *Journal of Child Psychology and Psychiatry*, 48(3-4), 2007). Responding to cries does not "spoil" infants — studies show that responsive caregiving leads to less crying over time, not more (Bell, S.M. & Ainsworth, M.D.S., "Infant Crying and Maternal Responsiveness," *Child Development*, 43(4), 1972). Research on the developmental timeline of self-regulation confirms that the neurological capacity for self-soothing does not exist in the first six months of life and develops gradually through the second year — not by withholding comfort, but through repeated cycles of co-regulation that the infant eventually internalizes (Kopp, C.B., "Antecedents of Self-Regulation: A Developmental Perspective," Developmental Psychology, 18(2), 1982). The distinction between self-soothing and self-suppression is clinically significant: an infant who stops signaling because they feel regulated is developing differently than one who stops signaling because they have learned that signals go unanswered (Tronick, E.Z., "Emotions and Emotional Communication in Infants," *American Psychologist*, 44(2), 1989).

On the limitations of prohibition in infancy: Research on infant cognitive development confirms that children under two cannot form the abstract connection between a prohibition and a category of danger — they respond to conditioned associations between a sound and a behavior, with no conceptual understanding underneath (Zelazo, P.D., Müller, U., Frye, D., & Marcovitch, S., "The Development of Executive Function in Early Childhood," *Monographs of the Society for Research in Child Development*, 68(3), 2003). Studies document that frequent negative commands can suppress exploratory behavior — a developmental necessity at this age — without building genuine understanding of risk (Belsky, J., Garduque, L., & Hrncir, E., "Assessing Performance, Competence, and Executive Capacity in Infant Play," *Developmental Psychology*, 20(3), 1984). Research supports redirection as more developmentally appropriate than prohibition for children under two, preserving the exploratory drive while managing safety (Kopp, C.B., "Regulation of Distress and Negative Emotions: A Developmental View," *Developmental Psychology*, 25(3), 1989).

On cultural variation in parenting: Cross-cultural research acknowledges significant variation in parenting practices across cultures, including sleep arrangements, feeding practices, and caregiver configurations (Keller, H., *Cultures of Infancy*, Erlbaum, 2007). Studies suggest that while specific practices vary, the underlying principles of responsive, consistent care appear to support healthy development across cultural contexts (Mesman, J., Van IJzendoorn, M.H., & Sagi-Schwartz, A., “Cross-Cultural Patterns of Attachment: Universal and Contextual Dimensions,” in *Handbook of Attachment*, 3rd ed., Guilford Press, 2016).

BOOK TWO:

When Words Arrive

A Field Guide for the Talking Years (2-5)

"Children are not things to be molded, but are people to be unfolded."

— Jess Lair

BOOK TWO CONTENTS

What's Actually Happening

One day, they pointed and grunted. The next day — or so it seems — they have *opinions*. Loud ones. About everything.

Welcome to the talking years.

Between ages two and five, your child's brain is doing something remarkable: it's building a language system from scratch. They'll go from a handful of words to thousands. From "more milk" to "why is the sky blue and also why can't I have ice cream for breakfast and also where do dogs go when they die?"

It's exhilarating. It's exhausting. It's also deeply, profoundly confusing — for both of you.

Here's what nobody tells you: **the fact that they can talk doesn't mean they can communicate**. Not the way you think. Not yet.

This is the central insight of *Why Won't You Listen?* — and it starts here, in these early talking years. Your child is building a language system, but it's not your language system. Not yet. They're constructing what we might call their own "word universe" — a place where words mean what *they* think they mean, where logic works differently, where time is a foreign concept, and where "no" is both their favorite word and the one they understand least when it comes from you.

Research shows that children this age hear and process language through developmental filters that adults have long since forgotten. What you say and what they receive are often two very different things.

This isn't a defect. It's development.

And understanding it will save you — and them — enormous frustration.

The Word Universe Gap

This gap — what *Why Won't You Listen?* calls the "word universe" — is where most parent-child friction lives.

Imagine you've just arrived in a foreign country. You've taken a few language classes. You can order coffee, ask for directions, maybe make small talk about the weather.

Now imagine someone starts explaining their tax situation to you. In rapid-fire speech. With idioms. And sarcasm. And they get frustrated when you don't follow.

That's roughly what it's like to be three years old.

Your child is building vocabulary at an astonishing rate — sometimes ten or more new words a day. But vocabulary isn't comprehension. They're collecting words like seashells on a beach, but they don't yet understand the ocean.

What this looks like in real life:

You say: "We're leaving in five minutes." They hear: Words. Some of them familiar. Nothing actionable.

You say: “If you don’t put on your shoes, we can’t go to the park.” They hear: “Shoes... park!” (The conditional logic — the *if/then* — doesn’t register.)

You say: “We don’t hit. Hitting hurts. How would you feel if someone hit you?” They hear: A lot of words, a question they can’t actually process, and your displeasure — which is the only part that registers clearly.

You say: “I’m disappointed in your choices.” They hear: “I’m disappointed in *you*.” (Abstract concepts like “choices” as separate from self don’t exist yet.)

This is the word universe gap. You’re speaking Adult — a language full of conditionals, abstractions, temporal concepts, and assumed context. They’re listening in Toddler — a language of concrete nouns, immediate experience, and emotional tone.

The gap isn’t a failure of attention. Research shows it’s a feature of development.

What Your Child's Brain Is Actually Doing

During these years, your child's brain is engaged in several massive construction projects simultaneously. Understanding these helps explain almost everything about their behavior.

LANGUAGE ACQUISITION. They're not just learning words — they're figuring out grammar, syntax, pronunciation, and pragmatics (how language works in social situations). This is computational work that would challenge a supercomputer, and they're doing it while also learning to use a fork.

SYMBOLIC THINKING. They're beginning to understand that things can represent other things. A banana can be a phone. A box can be a spaceship. The word "dog" can stand for actual dogs, pictures of dogs, stuffed dogs, and the concept of dog-ness in general. This is massive cognitive work — and it's the foundation of all later abstract thinking.

THEORY OF MIND (EMERGING). Research by Wellman and others shows that somewhere between three and five, children begin to understand that other people have thoughts and feelings different from their own. Before this clicks, they literally cannot understand that you don't know what they know, or that their desires aren't obvious to everyone. This is why "think about how your friend feels" is meaningless to a three-year-old — they can't yet do what you're asking.

EMOTIONAL DEVELOPMENT (EXPANDING BUT NOT REGULATED). The prefrontal cortex — the brain's "control center" — is under heavy construction. They have big feelings and almost no tools to manage them. The feelings come out as behavior because they don't have anywhere else to go.

EVERYTHING ELSE. They're also learning to run, climb, draw, use the toilet, make friends, navigate social rules, and understand a world that's constantly surprising them.

Given all this, it's remarkable they function at all. And yet we expect them to "listen" when we explain why they can't have a second cookie.

The Magical Thinking Years

Here's something that will help you understand roughly 80% of the baffling things your child does between ages two and five:
They live in a world where magic is real.

This isn't cute or quaint — it's how their brain actually works right now. Research on cognitive development shows that children this age don't yet distinguish clearly between fantasy and reality, between wishing and causing, between thoughts and events.

What magical thinking looks like:

- They believe that if they wish hard enough, something will happen
- They think their thoughts can cause events ("I was mad at Grandma and then she got sick — did I make her sick?")
- They believe monsters might actually be under the bed
- They think cartoon characters are real, or at least might be
- They believe you can see their dreams, or that dreams happened in real life
- They think the rules of pretend might apply to reality

Why this matters for communication:

When you say "there's no monster," you're using logic. They're not operating in logic. They're operating in a world where things that feel real *are* real. The fear is real, so the monster is real. Your rational explanation doesn't touch the fear — it just tells them you don't understand.

What helps:

Instead of logic, use the rules of their world. "Monster spray" (water in a spray bottle) works because it operates within magical thinking. Checking under the bed works. A stuffed animal "protector" works. You're not lying to them — you're speaking their language until their brain is ready for yours.

The accidental lies:

Magical thinking also explains why children this age "lie" without lying. When your three-year-old says they didn't eat the chocolate — while their face is covered in chocolate — they're not being defiant. In their mind, if they didn't *mean* to do wrong, or if they wish they hadn't done it, then in some sense they didn't do it.

This isn't moral failure. It's magical thinking meeting an uncomfortable reality. They'll grow out of it as their brain develops the capacity to distinguish between what they wish were true and what actually happened. Usually by age five or six, this begins to shift.

The "Why" Phase: What's Actually Happening

"Why is the sky blue?" "Why do dogs bark?" "Why can't I have ice cream?" "Why is that man walking?" "Why?" "Why?" "Why?"

Around age three, many children enter the "why" phase. It can feel relentless. It is relentless. But here's what research tells us is actually happening:

THEY'RE NOT TRYING TO ANNOY YOU. (Well, not usually.) They're building a mental model of how the world works. Every "why" is an attempt to understand cause and effect, motivation, and how things connect.

THEY'RE BUILDING THEORY OF MIND. Research shows that the "why" questions — especially about people ("why did she do that?") — are actually building the neural architecture for understanding that others have reasons, intentions, and perspectives. Those exhausting questions are crucial development.

THEY OFTEN DON'T WANT A REAL ANSWER. Sometimes "why" is a conversation-continuer. They want to keep talking to you. They want your attention. The question itself is connection-seeking.

What helps:

- Answer simply and concretely when you can
- Turn it back to them sometimes: “Why do you think?”
- Recognize when “why” means “keep talking to me” and respond to that need
- It’s okay to say “I don’t know — let’s wonder about that together”
- It’s also okay to say “My brain is tired of why questions right now. Let’s talk about something else.”

The why phase typically peaks between three and four and gradually subsides as their understanding of cause and effect becomes more sophisticated. It ends. Eventually. We promise.

The Development of Fear

Something strange happens around age two or three: new fears emerge that weren't there before.

The child who happily splashed in the bathtub suddenly becomes terrified of the drain. The toddler who loved dogs now screams when one approaches. Monsters, shadows, loud noises, the dark — fears seem to multiply just as your child becomes more capable in every other way.

This seems counterintuitive. But research shows it makes developmental sense.

Why fears increase at this age:

Their imagination is developing faster than their ability to reality-test. They can now imagine scary things — but they can't yet determine what's real and what isn't. Imagination without reality-testing equals fear.

They understand more about the world, including that bad things can happen. But they don't yet understand probability or their own safety. They know dogs can bite. They don't know that most dogs won't.

They're also becoming aware of their own smallness and vulnerability. The world is very big. They are very small. This is existentially terrifying when you think about it.

What helps:

- Take fears seriously without amplifying them. "You're scared of the drain. I understand. The drain can't hurt you, but I'll stay right here."
- Use their magical thinking constructively (monster spray, protective stuffed animals, special "brave" songs)
- Don't force exposure. Gradual, child-led approach to feared things works better than "just face it"
- Provide extra comfort and connection during fear phases
- Remember: this is a sign of cognitive development, not regression

What doesn't help:

- Dismissing: "Don't be silly, there's nothing to be scared of"
- Shaming: "Big kids aren't afraid of that"
- Logic (alone): "Monsters aren't real" doesn't help when they feel real
- Forcing: Making them confront the feared thing before they're ready

Most childhood fears at this age are temporary and will pass as their brain develops better reality-testing. If fears are severe, persistent, or significantly interfering with daily life, that's worth discussing with your pediatrician.

Social Development: From Parallel to Play

Watch two two-year-olds "playing together." You'll notice something interesting: they're usually not playing together at all. They're playing *near* each other. Same sandbox, different universes.

This is called parallel play, and it's completely normal and developmentally appropriate.

The progression research shows:

SOLITARY PLAY (0-2): Playing alone, not particularly interested in other children

PARALLEL PLAY (2-3): Playing alongside other children, same space, minimal interaction

ASSOCIATIVE PLAY (3-4): Interacting during play, sharing materials, but no coordinated goal

COOPERATIVE PLAY (4-5): Actually playing together with shared goals and coordinated roles

If your two-year-old isn't "playing well" with others, they're probably not developmentally ready to. This isn't a social skills problem — it's a timeline.

What this means practically:

- Playdates at age two are really for the parents. The kids are just parallel playing.
- Conflict is normal as they learn to share space and materials
- Taking turns is a skill that emerges gradually — expecting it too early leads to frustration
- Sharing is not intuitive. It's learned. And it's learned slowly.

The sharing myth:

We tell toddlers to share as if it should be obvious and easy. Research shows it's neither.

To share, a child must:

- Understand that others have desires (theory of mind — still developing)
- Control their own impulse to keep the thing (impulse control — barely exists)
- Trust that the toy will come back (object permanence is solid, but trust isn't)
- Value the other child's happiness (empathy — still in early stages)
- That's a lot to ask of a brain that can't yet understand "five minutes."

What helps:

- Parallel play is fine. Don't force interaction.
- Taking turns is easier than sharing (it has structure)
- Narrate the social situation: "Maya is playing with the truck now. When she's done, it can be your turn."
- Some things don't have to be shared. Special toys can be put away before playdates.
- Model sharing in your own life: "I'm sharing my snack with you. Sharing feels good."

“Me Do It!”: The Autonomy Imperative

Around age two, a new phrase enters your vocabulary. Not your child’s vocabulary — yours. You start thinking it, bracing for it, dreading it:

“Me do it!”

Also known as: “I do it myself!” “No help!” “MY turn!” and the ever-popular [screaming because you opened the banana they wanted to open themselves, and now the banana is ruined forever, and life is over].

This isn’t defiance. Research shows it’s a developmental imperative.

What’s happening:

Your child is individuating — becoming their own person, separate from you. To do this, they must assert themselves. They must say no. They must do things themselves. They must have opinions that differ from yours.

This is healthy. Essential, even. Children who don’t individuate have problems later. You want them to do this.

You just wish they didn’t have to do it during every single task that would take you thirty seconds and takes them forty-five minutes.

What helps:

- Build in extra time. Everything takes longer now. Accept it.
- Let them struggle a little. Resist the urge to swoop in.
- Offer help without taking over: "Can I hold this part while you do that part?"
- Give autonomy where you can so they don't have to fight for it: "Do you want to put your shoes on first or your jacket?"
- Pick your battles. Let them win the ones that don't matter.
- Praise the effort, not just the outcome: "You worked really hard on that zipper."

The independence paradox:

Here's the confusing part: they want independence AND they want you close. They want to do it themselves AND they need you to watch. They want autonomy AND they need security.

This isn't contradiction. It's healthy development. They're venturing out from the secure base (you) and returning to it. Out and back. Out and back. Just like in the earlier months when they were learning to crawl and walk.

Your job: be the base. Let them venture. Welcome them back.

Teaching new tasks: Tell, Show, Try, Do

When your toddler wants to "do it myself," that's an opportunity — if you know how to teach without taking over.

A simple framework that works:

TELL. Give simple, clear instruction. Not "get dressed" but "first we put our arms through the holes, then we pull it over our head." Break it into steps they can understand.

SHOW. Do it while they watch. No participation yet — just observation. This proves it can be done and shows them what it looks like.

TRY. Their turn. This is the hard part for parents: *let them struggle.* Don't jump in. Don't correct mid-attempt. Don't take over when it's going slowly. Questions are welcome. Help is not — unless they ask.

DO. Now it's theirs. With practice, they'll find their own way. Maybe they put pants on differently than you do. That's fine. Ownership matters more than your method.

Why this works:

Research shows that children often refuse tasks (or melt down during them) because they don't actually know how, or they're afraid of failing. This framework removes both barriers:

- TELL removes the unknown
- SHOW proves it's possible
- TRY makes failure safe (you're watching, not judging)
- DO gives them ownership and pride

When your 3-year-old insists on pouring their own milk and you're bracing for disaster — this is your roadmap. Tell them how. Show them once. Let them try (yes, there might be spilled milk). Then let them own it.

The messes are temporary. The competence lasts.

Toilet Training: A Developmental (Not Battle) View

We're not going to tell you how to toilet train your child. Every child is different, every family is different, and there are plenty of books devoted to the specifics.

What we'll tell you is what the research says about the developmental picture:

Readiness matters more than method. Studies consistently show that children trained earlier don't end up trained sooner — they just train longer. Starting when they're ready leads to faster, easier training.

Signs of readiness (usually between 2-3):

- Staying dry for longer periods
- Awareness of bodily sensations before they happen
- Interest in the toilet or underwear
- Ability to follow simple instructions
- Some ability to pull pants up and down
- Discomfort with wet or dirty diapers

What research tells us doesn't help:

- Pressure, shame, or punishment for accidents
- Starting before the child is ready
- Power struggles (you will lose — they control this body function)
- Comparing to other children's timelines

What research tells us does help:

- Waiting for readiness
- Matter-of-fact, non-shaming responses to accidents
- Patience (most children take several months to be fully reliable)
- Recognizing that regression during stress is normal

A word about timelines:

The average age of toilet training completion has increased over the past several decades — not because children have changed, but because we've learned more about readiness and development. If your pediatrician isn't concerned, you probably don't need to be either.

Sleep: Why It Gets Weird

You finally got the sleep thing figured out. They were sleeping through the night. Life was beautiful.

And then... they weren't.

Sleep often becomes more complicated between ages two and four. Research points to several developmental reasons:

IMAGINATION DEVELOPMENT. They can now imagine scary things — which means bedtime can become fear time. Darkness is scarier when you can imagine what might be in it.

FOMO (FEAR OF MISSING OUT). They're aware that life continues after they go to bed. You're still out there, doing things. Possibly fun things. This is outrageous and must be investigated.

TESTING LIMITS. If they've learned that bedtime can be negotiated, they'll negotiate. Every night. Relentlessly.

NIGHTMARES EMERGE. As imagination develops, so do bad dreams. Nightmares typically peak between ages three and six.

What helps:

- Consistent bedtime routine (predictability is calming)
- Addressing fears with their language (monster spray, etc.)
- Clear, firm limits with warm delivery
- A "bedtime pass" system (one ticket to leave the room for water/hug/bathroom, then no more)
- Nightlight if darkness is scary
- Comfort for nightmares without too much stimulation (calm, brief, boring)
- Making sure they're getting enough daytime physical activity

Night terrors vs. nightmares:

Night terrors (screaming, thrashing, seeming awake but not responsive) are different from nightmares. They happen during deep sleep, the child usually doesn't remember them, and the best approach is to keep them safe without trying to wake them fully. They're scary for parents but typically not distressing for the child, who has no memory of them.

If sleep problems are severe or persistent, your pediatrician can help rule out any underlying issues.

The Mismatch That Causes Most Conflicts

Here's where the frustration lives:

Parents think in language. Young children think in experience.

When you explain something to a young child, you're assuming that words carry meaning the way they do for you — that an explanation should produce understanding, and understanding should produce behavior change.

But for a child this age:

- Words are still somewhat magical and slippery
- Explanation doesn't equal comprehension
- Comprehension doesn't equal retention
- Retention doesn't equal impulse control
- And impulse control barely exists anyway

This is why you can explain — clearly, calmly, at their level — why we don't throw food, and five minutes later they're launching peas across the kitchen.

They're not defying you. They're not "testing" you (at least not the way you think). They're being *developmentally normal.*

The performance trap is in full effect now. They can say things they don't understand. They can repeat rules they can't follow. They can nod along while processing almost nothing. Their verbal ability dramatically outpaces their comprehension and their self-control.

This is the setup for the most common parent-child conflict pattern:

1. Child does something they've been told not to do
2. Parent assumes child understood and is being defiant
3. Parent escalates (frustration, consequences, lectures)
4. Child feels confused, scared, or ashamed — but doesn't know why
5. Connection erodes
6. Behavior gets worse (because behavior is communication)
7. Repeat

The way out of this cycle isn't more explaining. It isn't stricter consequences. Research suggests it's understanding what they actually can — and can't — do yet.

What Your Child Needs

SHORT SENTENCES. Really short. Like, shorter than you think. One idea at a time. Pause between ideas. Give them time to process. Their processing speed is not yours.

"Shoes on." (pause) "Then car." (pause) "Then park."

Not: "Okay sweetie, we need to get going soon, so I need you to put on your shoes so we can get in the car and go to the park, but first we need to find your jacket because it might be cold later."

CONCRETE LANGUAGE. Abstract words are noise. "Be good" means nothing. "Use gentle hands" means something. "Make good choices" is vapor. "You can pick the red cup or the blue cup" is solid ground.

CONNECTION BEFORE DIRECTION. This principle from *Why Won't You Listen?* applies especially here. Before you give an instruction, get connected: eye contact, physical proximity, sometimes a gentle touch. A child who feels connected is a child who can hear you. A child who feels disconnected is defended — and defended children can't process.

VALIDATION BEFORE CORRECTION. When they're upset, don't start with the lesson. Start with the feeling. "You really wanted that toy. You're disappointed." *Then,* once they feel felt, you can address the behavior. This isn't coddling. Research shows emotional flooding shuts down the learning brain.

PATIENCE WITH REPETITION. You will say the same thing a thousand times. This isn't failure — it's how brains learn at this age. They need repetition, consistency, and patience. The neural pathways are being built one repetition at a time.

ROUTINES AND PREDICTABILITY. Their world is chaotic and confusing. Routines give them something to hold onto. When things happen in predictable sequences, they feel safer. Transitions are hard because they represent loss of control — give warnings, use rituals, mark the moments.

PLAY. This is not optional. Play is how they process their world, practice social skills, work through fears, and connect with you. Get on the floor. Be the baby dragon they're slaying. Let them lead. This is relationship-building in their native language.

YOUR PRESENCE DURING BIG FEELINGS. They will have meltdowns. Big ones. Public ones. Ones that make you question your life choices. Your job isn't to stop the feeling or fix the situation. Your job is to stay calm (or fake it), stay close, and help them ride it out. "You're really upset. I'm here. We'll get through this together."

What It Looks Like When It's Working

- Language is exploding — new words appearing constantly, sentences getting longer
- They can follow simple, concrete instructions (when they want to)
- Tantrums happen but don't last forever, and they recover with your help
- Imaginative play is rich and engaging
- They seek you out to share excitement, show you things, include you
- They're beginning to recognize emotions in others — noticing when someone is sad or hurt, even if they can't yet understand why or what to do about it
- They can sometimes wait, sometimes share, sometimes manage small frustrations
- They apologize (even if they don't fully understand why)
- Connection repairs happen — after conflict, you find your way back to each other
- They're curious, questioning, exploring

Notice what's not on this list: perfect compliance. Consistent listening. Rational responses to reasonable requests.

Those aren't realistic expectations for this age. If you're expecting them, you'll be frustrated. If you're not, you'll be able to appreciate what's actually developing — which is remarkable.

What It Looks Like When Support Is Needed

Every child develops differently. Research shows wide variation in what's typical. These aren't diagnostic criteria — just signals that a conversation with your pediatrician might be helpful:

- Very few words by age 2, or not combining words by age 2.5
- Doesn't respond to their name consistently
- Limited eye contact or interest in social interaction
- No pretend play by age 3
- Speech that's very difficult for strangers to understand by age 3-4
- Significant regression — losing skills they previously had
- Tantrums that are extremely prolonged, frequent, or intense beyond what seems typical
- Persistent difficulty with transitions that doesn't improve over time
- You feel consistently unable to connect, or something just feels "off"

Early intervention makes a significant difference. If your gut says something's worth checking, check it. You're not overreacting. You're paying attention.

The Discipline Question

Let's address this directly, because it's probably on your mind.

This book isn't a discipline manual. We're not going to tell you which consequences work best or how to implement time-outs effectively or whether to spank (please don't) or use reward charts (they're complicated).

What we'll tell you is this: **research shows that most discipline struggles at this age are actually development in action**.

The child who "won't listen" often can't listen — not the way you mean. The child who "defies" you often doesn't understand what you're asking, even if they can repeat what you say. The child who "keeps doing it anyway" often lacks the impulse control to stop. The child who "should know better by now" developmentally isn't there yet.

This doesn't mean behavior doesn't matter. It doesn't mean you let them run wild. What the research suggests is that adjusting expectations to match what's actually possible — and responding to the child in front of you rather than the child you think they should be — changes everything.

Practical implications:

- **Redirect more than correct.** When they're headed toward trouble, guide them somewhere else rather than explaining why the trouble is troublesome.
- **Make the environment work for you.** Childproofing isn't giving up — it's wisdom. Remove what you don't want them to touch rather than constantly saying no.
- **Keep consequences immediate and simple.** "You threw the truck, so I'm putting the truck away." That's it. No lecture. They can't process the lecture anyway.
- **Prioritize connection over compliance.** A connected child is a cooperative child. If you're in constant power struggles, the relationship needs attention.
- **Remember: they're not giving you a hard time. They're having a hard time.** Respond to what's underneath the behavior, not just the behavior itself.

Screens: A Brief Word

We're not here to lecture you about screen time. You're tired. Screens buy you twenty minutes to make dinner or take a shower or just breathe. We get it.

What research tells us:

CONTENT MATTERS MORE THAN TIME (within reason). Educational, slow-paced programming is different from fast-paced, frenetic content.

CO-VIEWING HELPS. Watching with them and talking about what you see transforms passive consumption into interactive learning.

DISPLACEMENT IS THE CONCERN. The question isn't just "is screen time bad?" but "what is screen time replacing?" If it's replacing sleep, physical activity, or human interaction, that's a problem.

TRANSITIONS OFF SCREENS ARE HARD. Their brains are in a stimulation loop. Give warnings. Have rituals for transitioning off. Expect some resistance.

YOUR SCREEN USE MATTERS TOO. They're watching you. If you're constantly on your phone, that's what they learn attention looks like.

There's no perfect number of minutes. There's no magic app that solves everything. Use your judgment. Pay attention to your child's behavior before, during, and after screens. Adjust accordingly.

Simple Connection Builders (2–5 Years)

SPECIAL TIME. Ten to fifteen minutes a day of one-on-one, child-led play. No teaching. No correcting. No phones. Just you, fully present, following their lead. This fills their connection tank like nothing else.

SPORTSCASTING. Narrate what they're doing without judgment. "You're building a tall tower. Now you're putting the red block on top." This makes them feel seen and builds language simultaneously.

EMOTION LABELING. Name their feelings before they can. "You look frustrated." "That made you really happy!" "You're disappointed we can't stay longer." You're building their emotional vocabulary — the words they'll eventually use instead of screaming.

SILLY PLAY. Be ridiculous. Chase them slowly like a bumbling monster. Pretend to fall asleep and snore loudly. Make the stuffed animals talk in funny voices. Laughter is bonding. And they're funny — genuinely funny — if you let yourself notice.

READING TOGETHER. Not for education (though that happens). For closeness. For ritual. For the comfort of your voice and the shared attention and the conversation that emerges. Let them pick the same book forty times. That's not tedium — that's trust.

SIMPLE CHOICES. "Do you want the red cup or the blue cup?" "Should we read the bear book or the truck book?" Choices give them power in a world where they control very little. Just limit the options — too many choices overwhelm.

PHYSICAL AFFECTION. Hugs, cuddles, gentle roughhousing, piggyback rides — physical connection is primary at this age. Some kids need more than others. Pay attention to what yours seeks.

REPAIR RITUALS. After conflict, find your way back. "We had a hard moment. I got frustrated and you got upset. But we're okay now. I love you." They need to know the relationship survives rupture.

ENTER THEIR WORLD. Their imaginative world is rich and real to them. When they invite you into their pretend game, go. Be the customer at their restaurant. Be the patient for their doctor kit. This is them sharing their inner life with you.

A Word for the Exhausted Parent

They ask "why" forty-seven times before breakfast. They take twenty minutes to put on shoes that they'll then refuse to wear. They melt down because you cut the sandwich the wrong way — and no, you cannot uncut it, and yes, this is apparently a tragedy of historic proportions.

They have opinions about socks. Strong opinions. Life-or-death sock opinions.

This age is relentless in a way that's hard to describe to anyone who hasn't lived it.

Here's what might help:

THIS IS TEMPORARY. Not in the distant, abstract sense — in the real sense. The particular exhaustions of this age will give way to the particular exhaustions of the next age. The "why" phase ends. The shoe battles evolve. The sandwich meltdowns become something else. This specific hard is not forever.

THEY'RE SUPPOSED TO BE IRRATIONAL. That's not a flaw in your parenting. That's where they are developmentally. You're not failing because they're not reasonable. They *can't* be reasonable yet. Their brain isn't built for it.

YOU DON'T HAVE TO LOVE EVERY MOMENT. You can adore your child and also desperately need them to stop talking for five minutes. Both things can be true simultaneously. The pressure to treasure every second is a lie. Some seconds are just survival.

YOUR FRUSTRATION IS INFORMATION, NOT FAILURE. When you're consistently at the end of your rope, that's a signal — not that you're bad at this, but that you need more support. More breaks. More help. More sleep. More something.

CONNECTION COMPOUNDS. Every moment of genuine presence — every time you get on the floor, make eye contact, play the silly game, stay calm during the storm — it's adding up. You won't see the results immediately. That's not how it works. But the architecture is being built. The relationship is being wired. The foundation is being laid.

What you're doing matters, even when it doesn't feel like it.

Especially when it doesn't feel like it.

The Mirror: Your Private Reflection

For your eyes only.

The way we communicate with our children is often shaped by how we were communicated with. Sometimes we're repeating what we knew. Sometimes we're running from it. Usually, we're doing some of both — without quite realizing it.

These questions aren't about judgment. They're about awareness.

About Your Own Childhood (ages 2-5):

1. When you were young and didn't understand something, how did your parents typically respond?
   - Patient explanation
   - Frustration ("I already told you")
   - Dismissal ("You'll understand when you're older")
   - Anger
   - I don't remember

2. When you expressed big emotions as a young child, what happened?
    - Comfort and acceptance
    - “Stop crying or I’ll give you something to cry about”
    - Sent away until you calmed down
    - Ignored
    - Mocked or shamed
    - I don’t remember
3. How were your “why” questions received?
    - Welcomed and engaged
    - Tolerated briefly, then shut down
    - Treated as annoyance
    - I learned not to ask
4. How was your need for independence handled?
    - Encouraged and supported
    - Seen as defiance to be corrected
    - Ignored — you were expected to comply
    - It varied unpredictably
5. What phrase or tone from your childhood still echoes in your head — for better or worse?
6. What do you wish your parents had understood about you at this age?

About Your Parenting Now:

7. When your child doesn't "listen," your first internal reaction is usually:
    - Curiosity (what's going on for them?)
    - Frustration (why won't they just do what I ask?)
    - Anxiety (what am I doing wrong?)
    - Patience (this is normal for their age)
    - Overwhelm (I don't know how to handle this)
8. How often do you find yourself explaining things in ways you later realize were too complex for their age?
9. What's your go-to response when they're having a meltdown?
10. Is there a phrase you say that sounds like someone from your past — and how do you feel when you hear yourself say it?
11. When do you feel most connected to your child? When do you feel most disconnected?
12. What's one thing you're doing well that you want to keep doing?
13. What's one thing you want to do differently?

A Note on These Reflections

If these questions surfaced difficult memories — if you recognized patterns you don't want to repeat, or felt grief for understanding you didn't receive — that's normal. It's also useful.

You can give what you didn't get. It requires more intention, more effort, and often more support than parenting on autopilot. But it's possible. Parents do it every day.

The parent who was dismissed can learn to validate. The parent who was silenced can learn to welcome questions. The parent who was shamed can learn to accept big feelings. The parent whose independence was crushed can learn to encourage autonomy.

Not perfectly. Not without slipping into old patterns sometimes. But enough. Good enough.

That's all it takes.

The Research Behind These Words

For clinicians, educators, researchers and those who want to verify the claims: full citations for claims made in each section follow. This book is designed to be recommended to clients and families as an accessible entry point to developmental research.

On language development: Research documents that children acquire language at a remarkable rate during ages 2-5, often learning multiple new words daily (Hart, B. & Risley, T.R., *Meaningful Differences in the Everyday Experience of Young American Children*, Brookes Publishing, 1995). Studies show that vocabulary size and language exposure during this period predict later academic outcomes (Hoff, E., "The Specificity of Environmental Influence: Socioeconomic Status Affects Early Vocabulary Development via Maternal Speech," *Child Development*, 74(5), 2003). However, vocabulary acquisition outpaces comprehension — children can say words they don't fully understand, a phenomenon documented across developmental linguistics research (Clark, E.V., *First Language Acquisition*, Cambridge University Press, 2009).

On the word universe gap: Research in developmental psycholinguistics confirms that children process language differently than adults (Hirsh-Pasek, K. & Golinkoff, R.M., *How Babies Talk: The Magic and Mystery of Language in the First Three Years of Life*, Dutton, 1999). Studies show that young children struggle with conditional logic ("if/then" statements), temporal concepts, and abstract language (Bloom, L. & Lahey, M., *Language Development and Language Disorders*, Wiley, 1978). What adults intend to communicate and what children actually receive are often significantly different — a gap that narrows gradually through childhood but persists longer than most parents expect (Palincsar, A.S., "The Role of Dialogue in Providing Scaffolded Instruction," *Educational Psychologist*, 21(1-2), 1986).

On theory of mind: Pioneering research established that theory of mind — understanding that others have different thoughts, knowledge, and beliefs — develops significantly between ages 3-5 (Wellman, H.M., *Making Minds: How Theory of Mind Develops*, Oxford University Press, 2014). Classic "false belief" tasks demonstrate this development (Wimmer, H. & Perner, J., "Beliefs About Beliefs: Representation and Constraining Function of Wrong Beliefs in Young Children's Understanding of Deception," *Cognition*, 13(1), 1983). Before theory of mind is established, children literally cannot understand that you don't know what they know, which explains many communication failures during this period (Flavell, J.H., "Cognitive Development: Children's Knowledge About the Mind," *Annual Review of Psychology*, 50, 1999).

On magical thinking: Piaget's foundational research documented that children ages 2-7 are in the "preoperational stage," characterized by magical thinking, egocentrism, and difficulty distinguishing fantasy from reality (Piaget, J., *The Child's Conception of the World*, Routledge & Kegan Paul, 1929). Children this age may believe thoughts can cause events, that wishing makes things happen, and that imagined threats are real (Woolley, J.D., "Thinking About Fantasy: Are Children Fundamentally Different Thinkers and Believers from Adults?" *Child Development*, 68(6), 1997). This is normal cognitive development, not confusion or deficiency.

On the "why" phase: Research shows that the relentless "why" questioning typical of ages 3-4 serves crucial developmental functions: building causal understanding, developing theory of mind, and maintaining social connection (Chouinard, M.M., "Children's Questions: A Mechanism for Cognitive Development," *Monographs of the Society for Research in Child Development*, 72(1), 2007). Studies suggest these questions are essential for cognitive development, particularly questions about people's motivations which build social understanding (Frazier, B.N., Gelman, S.A., & Wellman, H.M., "Preschoolers' Search for Explanatory Information Within Adult-Child Conversation," *Child Development*, 80(6), 2009).

On fear development: Research documents a predictable increase in fears during ages 2-4, coinciding with imagination development (Muris, P., Merckelbach, H., Ollendick, T.H., King, N.J., & Bogie, N., "Children's Nighttime Fears: Parent-Child Ratings of Frequency, Content, Origins, Coping Behaviors and Severity," *Behaviour Research and Therapy*, 39(1), 2001). Children can now imagine threats but lack the cognitive capacity to reality-test them. Studies show that fears at this age are typically transient and resolve as the brain develops better distinction between fantasy and reality (Gullone, E., "The Development of Normal Fear: A Century of Research," *Clinical Psychology Review*, 20(4), 2000).

On play development: Research established the progression from solitary play through parallel play (playing alongside but not with others) to associative and cooperative play (Parten, M.B., "Social Participation Among Preschool Children," *Journal of Abnormal and Social Psychology*, 27(3), 1932). Studies consistently show that parallel play — often misinterpreted as poor social skills — is developmentally normal for 2-3 year olds (Rubin, K.H., Bukowski, W.M., & Parker, J.G., "Peer Interactions, Relationships, and Groups," *Handbook of Child Psychology*, 6th ed., Wiley, 2006). True cooperative play typically emerges around age 4-5.

On sharing and social development: Research confirms that sharing requires multiple cognitive capacities still developing in young children: theory of mind, impulse control, trust, and empathy (Brownell, C.A., Svetlova, M., & Nichols, S., "To Share or Not to Share: When Do Toddlers Respond to Another's Needs?" *Infancy,* 14(1), 2009). Studies show that expecting robust sharing before age 3-4 is developmentally unrealistic. Turn-taking (which has clear structure) is easier to learn than sharing (which requires relinquishing without guarantee of return) (Hay, D.F., "Prosocial Development," *Journal of Child Psychology and Psychiatry*, 35(1), 1994).

On autonomy and individuation: Erikson's developmental framework identifies ages 2-3 as the stage of "autonomy vs. shame and doubt" (Erikson, E.H., *Childhood and Society*, W.W. Norton, 1950). Research supports that the drive for independence ("me do it!") is essential for healthy development. Studies show that children who are allowed appropriate autonomy develop better self-regulation and confidence than those whose independence is consistently thwarted (Deci, E.L. & Ryan, R.M., "The 'What' and 'Why' of Goal Pursuits: Human Needs and the Self-Determination of Behavior," *Psychological Inquiry*, 11(4), 2000).

On toilet training: Meta-analyses of toilet training research show that readiness-based approaches (waiting for developmental signs) result in faster completion than early training (Blum, N.J., Taubman, B., & Nemeth, N., "Relationship Between Age at Initiation of Toilet Training and Duration of Training: A Prospective Study," *Pediatrics*, 111(4), 2003). Studies consistently find that pressure, shame, and punishment delay rather than accelerate training and can cause lasting difficulties (Brazelton, T.B., "A Child-Oriented Approach to Toilet Training," *Pediatrics*, 29(1), 1962). The average age of toilet training completion has increased as understanding of developmental readiness has improved.

On sleep changes: Research documents predictable sleep disruptions during ages 2-4, linked to imagination development (fears), cognitive development (FOMO, awareness of continued activity), and limit-testing (Mindell, J.A. & Owens, J.A., *A Clinical Guide to Pediatric Sleep: Diagnosis and Management of Sleep Problems*, Lippincott Williams & Wilkins, 2015). Studies show that nightmares typically peak between ages 3-6 as imagination develops (Simard, V., Nielsen, T.A., Tremblay, R.E., Boivin, M., & Montplaisir, J.Y., "Longitudinal Study of Bad Dreams in Preschool-Aged Children," *Child Development*, 79(4), 2008). Consistent routines and addressing fears within the child's developmental framework are supported interventions.

On discipline and development: Research consistently shows that most "misbehavior" in young children reflects developmental limitations rather than defiance (Siegel, D.J. & Bryson, T.P., *No-Drama Discipline: The Whole-Brain Way to Calm the Chaos and Nurture Your*

Child's Developing Mind, Bantam, 2014). Studies document that impulse control depends on prefrontal cortex development, which is far from complete at this age (Diamond, A., "Executive Functions," *Annual Review of Psychology*, 64, 2013). Understanding this neurological reality shifts discipline approaches from punishment toward developmental accommodation.

On the performance-comprehension gap: Research confirms that children's verbal production (what they can say) significantly outpaces their comprehension (what they understand) and their behavioral capacity (what they can consistently do) (Bates, E., Dale, P.S., & Thal, D., "Individual Differences and Their Implications for Theories of Language Development," *The Handbook of Child Language*, Blackwell, 1995). Studies show children can repeat rules they cannot follow, nod along to instructions they don't understand, and appear to comprehend far more than they actually do (Flavell, J.H., Miller, P.H., & Miller, S.A., *Cognitive Development*, 4th ed., Prentice Hall, 2002).

On connection and compliance: Research in attachment theory and developmental psychology shows that children who feel securely connected to caregivers are more cooperative and easier to guide than those who feel disconnected (Bowlby, J., *A Secure Base: Parent-Child Attachment and Healthy Human Development*, Basic Books, 1988). Studies support "connection before correction" approaches — addressing the relationship before addressing behavior (Siegel, D.J. & Hartzell, M., *Parenting from the Inside Out: How a Deeper Self-Understanding Can Help You Raise Children Who Thrive*, Tarcher/Penguin, 2003).

On screen time: Research on screen use in young children is evolving. Current evidence suggests that content quality matters more than duration, co-viewing improves outcomes, and displacement (what screen time replaces) is a key concern (Christakis, D.A., "The Effects of Infant Media Usage: What Do We Know and What Should We Learn?" *Acta Paediatrica*, 98(1), 2009). Studies show that fast-paced content may affect attention development (Lillard, A.S. & Peterson, J., "The Immediate Impact of Different Types of Television on Young Children's Executive Function," *Pediatrics*, 128(4), 2011), and that transitions off screens are difficult due to the stimulation patterns involved (Radesky, J.S., Schumacher, J., & Zuckerman, B., "Mobile and Interactive Media Use by Young Children: The Good, the Bad, and the Unknown," *Pediatrics*, 135(1), 2015).

On empathy development: Research shows that empathy develops gradually through early childhood (Hoffman, M.L., *Empathy and Moral Development: Implications for Caring and Justice*, Cambridge University Press, 2000). Children ages 2-4 may recognize emotions in others but cannot yet fully understand or respond to others' emotional states (Wellman, H.M., Harris, P.L., Banerjee, M., & Sinclair, A., "Early Understanding of Emotion: Evidence from Natural Language," *Cognition and Emotion*, 9(2-3), 1995). True empathic response — understanding and sharing another's feelings — continues developing through middle childhood.

On emotional regulation: Research documents that the prefrontal cortex — responsible for impulse control and emotional regulation — is under active development during early childhood and won't be fully mature until the mid-twenties (Casey, B.J., Giedd, J.N., & Thomas, K.M., "Structural and Functional Brain Development and Its Relation to Cognitive Development," *Biological Psychology*, 54(1-3), 2000). Studies show that young children cannot regulate emotions independently and require co-regulation from caregivers to learn these skills (Calkins, S.D. & Hill, A., "Caregiver Influences on Emerging Emotion Regulation: Biological and Environmental Transactions in Early Development," *Handbook of Emotion Regulation*, Guilford Press, 2007).

BOOK THREE:

The Age of Reason

A Field Guide for the Thinking Years (5-7)

"Children have never been very good at listening to their elders, but they have never failed to imitate them."

— James Baldwin

BOOK THREE CONTENTS

What's Actually Happening

Something shifts around age five. You might not notice it at first — it's not as dramatic as first words or first steps. But somewhere in these years, the child you've been raising starts to... think differently.

They ask different questions. Not just "why is the sky blue?" but "what happens when you die?" and "is God real?" and "why do some people not have houses?"

They argue differently. Not just "I don't want to!" but "That's not fair because yesterday you said..." and "But the rule is..." and "You're not being logical."

They see differently. The magical thinking that defined their earlier years is giving way to something new — the beginning of reason, logic, and a hunger to understand how things actually work.

Welcome to what researchers call the **"5-to-7 shift"** — a fundamental reorganization of how your child's brain processes the world.

This transition has been recognized across cultures and throughout history. It's why formal schooling traditionally begins around this age. It's why many legal and religious traditions mark age seven as a threshold of accountability. It's why your child suddenly seems more capable of real conversation — and more capable of driving you crazy with their relentless logic.

Research shows that the brain reaches approximately its adult size by age seven. But size isn't the story — organization is. The neural connections are being refined, pruned, and strengthened. The capacity for sustained attention is developing. The prefrontal cortex is coming online in new ways.

Their body is changing too. They're losing baby teeth and growing adult ones — a visible marker of the transition they're experiencing internally. Coordination improves. Energy seems boundless (and sometimes exhausting to witness). They can run faster, climb higher, write smaller, and sit still longer than they could at four — though "longer" is relative.

Your child is crossing a threshold from the magical world of early childhood into something new — the beginning of the rational mind.

This is exciting. It's also disorienting — for both of you.

The In-Between

Here's what makes this age uniquely challenging: they're caught between two worlds.

They're not little anymore. They can dress themselves, make their own breakfast, read books, have real opinions, engage in actual conversation. They seem so capable.

But they're not big either. They still need you desperately — for comfort, for guidance, for help processing a world that's suddenly gotten much larger and more complicated. They still believe in Santa (maybe). They still have nightmares. They still fall apart sometimes in ways that seem "babyish."

They know they're supposed to be more grown up. They feel the expectation — from school, from peers, from you. And sometimes that expectation lands before the capacity arrives.

This is the gap of middle childhood: the expectation of maturity meeting the reality of still-developing brains.

Your child may ricochet between startlingly mature observations and complete meltdowns. Between independence and clinginess. Between "I can do it myself" and "I need you."

This isn't regression. This is the in-between. It's exhausting for them and confusing for you. But it's normal.

They need you to hold both truths: they're growing up, *and* they're still a child. They need more independence, *and* they need to know you're still their secure base.

School Changes Everything

If they weren't already in school, they are now. And school changes the developmental picture dramatically.

A NEW AUTHORITY ENTERS THEIR LIFE. The teacher becomes a significant figure — sometimes idealized, sometimes quoted at home with more reverence than you'd like. "My teacher says..." becomes a phrase you'll hear constantly. This can sting, but it's healthy. They're learning that trustworthy adults exist beyond their family.

PERFORMANCE BECOMES VISIBLE. For the first time, your child is being measured — reading levels, math groups, grades, assessments. They know where they stand relative to peers. This is the beginning of academic identity, for better or worse.

THE SOCIAL WORLD EXPANDS. Classmates become a daily reality. Friendships form, shift, break, reform. Social dynamics that you can't see or control are shaping your child's experience of themselves.

STRUCTURE REPLACES FLOW. The relatively unstructured days of early childhood give way to schedules, expectations, homework, and the need to sit still and pay attention for hours at a time. This is a significant regulatory demand on a still-developing brain.

What this means for you:

You're no longer the only — or even the primary — influence on their daily experience. You hear about their day secondhand (if you're lucky). You can't protect them from every social slight or academic frustration. You have to trust teachers, systems, and your child's own developing resilience.

This is hard. It's also necessary. Your job is shifting from direct management to coaching, supporting, and being the safe place they return to.

The Homework Reality

Let's name it: homework is often a battleground at this age.

They're tired after a full day of school. Their attention is spent. They want to play, not do more work. And yet — there it is. Worksheets. Reading logs. Spelling words.

What research suggests:

The evidence on homework effectiveness for young children is mixed at best. What seems to matter more than the homework itself is whether it becomes a source of chronic conflict or a manageable routine.

What helps:

- **ROUTINE OVER WILLPOWER.** Same time, same place, same sequence. Make it predictable so it doesn't require a daily negotiation.
- **STAY CLOSE BUT DON'T TAKE OVER.** Be available, not hovering. Help them get unstuck, don't do it for them.
- **KEEP PERSPECTIVE.** A six-year-old struggling with homework isn't failing at life. They're six.

- **COMMUNICATE WITH TEACHERS.** If homework is consistently taking far longer than expected or causing major distress, that's information the teacher needs.

The goal isn't perfect homework. It's building the habit of completing responsibilities — imperfectly, with support, over time.

Teaching new tasks: Why "I don't know how" is often fear in disguise

When children this age refuse a task or do it poorly, parents often assume laziness or defiance. But research suggests something else is frequently at play: **fear of failure** or **genuinely not knowing how** — even when they've been told.

Being told isn't the same as knowing.

A framework that addresses this:

TELL. Give clear, specific instruction. Not "clean your room" (overwhelming and vague) but "first put all the clothes in the hamper, then put the books on the shelf, then make the bed."

SHOW. Do the task while they watch. Start to finish, no participation yet. This is crucial — it proves the task is possible and shows what "done" looks like. Many children resist tasks because they genuinely can't picture the outcome.

TRY. Their turn. You observe. This is where parents often fail: they jump in to correct, to help, to speed things up. Resist. Let them struggle. Let them do it imperfectly. Questions are welcome. Takeovers are not.

DO. Now it's their task. With practice comes competence. With ownership comes pride. Encourage them to find their own method, their own efficiency. "You found a faster way to do that" matters more than "you did it exactly like I showed you."

Why this works:

- **TELL** removes the fear of the unknown
- **SHOW** removes the “I can’t” belief
- **TRY** makes failure safe — they’re learning, not performing
- **DO** transfers ownership — it’s their task now, not yours

When a child says “I don’t know how” for the tenth time, or does a task so poorly you suspect sabotage — consider whether all four stages actually happened. Often, one was skipped. And the missing stage is usually TRY: they were never allowed to struggle safely.

The Logic Trap

Here's where parents get fooled — and where frustration builds:

They seem so logical now. But the logic is partial.

Your 6-year-old can follow a rule. They can understand cause and effect. They can make an argument (oh, can they make an argument). They can reason their way through a problem.

So naturally, you start reasoning with them more. Explaining. Debating. Assuming that if you just lay out the logic clearly enough, they'll get it.

And sometimes they do. But often they don't — not because they're being difficult, but because their logic has limits they can't see.

What research tells us:

Children in the concrete operational stage (roughly 7-11) can think logically about *concrete* things — objects, events, experiences they've had. But they still struggle with:

- **ABSTRACT CONCEPTS** — "responsibility," "consequences," "respect" are still fuzzy
- **HYPOTHETICALS** — "What would happen if..." is harder than it seems

- **MULTIPLE PERSPECTIVES SIMULTANEOUSLY** — they can take your perspective OR theirs, but holding both is hard
- **LONG TIME HORIZONS** — "this will matter for your future" is almost meaningless

The communication gap continues — it just looks different.

The gap we explore in *Why Won't You Listen? The Science of What Kids Really Hear When You Speak* — what that book calls the "word universe" — continues at this age. In the toddler years, they couldn't process your words because they lacked vocabulary and impulse control. Now they have the words. They can even repeat your logic back to you. But the gap between *understanding your argument* and *being able to act on it consistently* is still significant.

They will nod along to your reasonable explanation about why they need to do homework before screens, and then argue about it again tomorrow as if the conversation never happened. This isn't defiance. Their brain is still building the architecture for consistent application of understood principles.

What helps:

- Keep expectations concrete and specific, not abstract
- Don't over-explain. State the expectation, follow through, move on.
- Expect to repeat yourself. Still. A lot.
- Pick your logical battles. Not everything requires a debate.

The Lying Question: What's Really Happening When They Don't Tell the Truth

Few things trigger parents like catching their child in a lie.

It feels like betrayal. It feels like a character flaw emerging. It feels like the beginning of something terrible — *What kind of person is my child becoming? Where did I go wrong?*

Take a breath. Here's what the research actually shows:

Lying is a cognitive achievement.

That's not a typo. Developmental psychologists have studied lying extensively, and the findings are counterintuitive: the ability to lie skillfully is a sign of healthy brain development.

Here's why:

To lie effectively, a child must:

- Understand that other people have different knowledge than they do (theory of mind)

- Hold two realities in their head simultaneously (what actually happened and what they're saying)
- Predict how their words will affect someone else's beliefs
- Plan and execute a coherent alternative narrative
- Regulate their expression and body language

These are sophisticated cognitive skills. Research shows that children who develop theory of mind earlier tend to lie earlier — and children with developmental delays in social cognition often lie later or less skillfully.

This doesn't mean lying is good. It means it's normal.

Almost all children lie. Studies suggest that by age 4, most children have attempted deception. By age 6, they're getting better at it. By age 7 or 8, their lies become harder to detect.

If your child is lying, their brain is doing exactly what developing brains do.

Why they lie at this age:

Understanding the *reason* behind the lie helps you respond appropriately:

TO AVOID PUNISHMENT. This is the most common reason. "Did you hit your sister?" "No." They know they did something wrong. They know consequences are coming. The lie is an attempt to escape. This is self-protective, not malicious.

TO AVOID DISAPPOINTING YOU. Sometimes children lie because your approval matters desperately to them. "Did you finish your homework?" "Yes." They didn't — but they couldn't bear to see your face fall. This lie comes from love, not contempt.

TO GET SOMETHING THEY WANT. "Mom said I could have a cookie." (Mom said no such thing.) This is wish fulfillment dressed as fact. They want the cookie so badly that the lie emerges almost automatically.

TO EXPERIMENT WITH POWER. Around this age, children discover that words can create reality. They can say something and make you believe it. This is heady stuff. Some lying is simply testing this new superpower.

To protect their inner world. As we discussed earlier, children are developing interiority — a private mental life. Sometimes lies are simply: "This is mine. You don't get to know everything about me." This is actually healthy individuation, even when the method is problematic.

TO AVOID SHAME. Different from avoiding punishment — this is about protecting their sense of self. "Did you wet the bed?" "No." The lie protects them from feeling humiliated, not from consequences.

The lying trap:

Here's something many parents don't realize: **the way you ask questions can invite lying**.

"Did you take a cookie?" (when you know they did) "Were you the one who broke this?" (when you saw them do it) "Did you brush your teeth?" (when you know they didn't)

These aren't questions. They're tests. And they put your child in an impossible position: tell the truth and face consequences, or lie and maybe escape.

Research suggests that **trap-setting increases lying**. When children learn that admitting the truth leads to punishment, they become more motivated to lie — and better at it.

What helps:

DON'T ASK QUESTIONS YOU ALREADY KNOW THE ANSWER TO. Instead of "Did you take a cookie?" try "I see you took a cookie. We talked about asking first." You've addressed the behavior without inviting a lie.

MAKE TRUTH-TELLING SAFER THAN LYING. If your child admits wrongdoing, acknowledge the courage that took before addressing the behavior. "Thank you for telling me the truth. That was hard. Now let's talk about what happened."

KEEP CONSEQUENCES PROPORTIONATE. If the punishment for lying is severe and the punishment for the original offense is also severe, you've created maximum incentive to lie. Consider: what's more important — punishing this moment or building long-term honesty?

RESPOND TO THE REASON, NOT JUST THE LIE. A child lying to avoid shame needs a different response than a child lying to manipulate. Look underneath.

DON'T CATASTROPHIZE. A 6-year-old who lies about taking a cookie is not on a path to becoming a con artist. They're being six. Respond to the developmental reality.

MODEL HONESTY — INCLUDING ABOUT YOUR OWN MISTAKES. "I told Grandma we were busy Saturday, but actually I just didn't feel like going. That wasn't honest of me. I should have said what I really felt."

TEACH THE VALUE OF TRUST, NOT JUST THE RULE AGAINST LYING. "When you tell me things that aren't true, it makes it harder for me to believe you next time. Trust is like that — it builds slowly and breaks quickly."

What doesn't help:

- Harsh punishment that makes truth-telling feel dangerous
- Shaming ("I can't believe you lied to me. What kind of person does that?")
- Setting traps and then punishing them for falling in
- Demanding confessions
- Long lectures about honesty
- Treating every lie as equally serious

The long view:

Your goal isn't to raise a child who never lies — that child doesn't exist. Your goal is to raise a child who:

- Understands why honesty matters
- Feels safe enough to tell the truth most of the time
- Develops integrity over time

This happens through relationship, not punishment. Through safety, not fear. Through your response to their lies being firm but not devastating.

They're not morally corrupt. They're developing. Meet them there.

Friendship and the Social Universe

Something profound happens in these years: **peers become central**.

Until now, your child's social world was mostly managed by you — playdates you arranged, activities you chose, conflicts you mediated. That's changing.

Friendships become personal, chosen, and emotionally significant. Your child will have a "best friend" (who may change weekly). They'll experience loyalty, jealousy, betrayal, and reconciliation — sometimes all before lunch.

What research shows about social development at this age:

- Children begin to compare themselves to peers in earnest
- Social hierarchies start to form (who's popular, who's not)
- Same-gender friendships typically dominate
- "Fairness" becomes an obsession — everything is measured and compared
- Rejection and exclusion are felt deeply and remembered

The fairness obsession:

"That's not fair!" is the anthem of this age. And they don't mean it philosophically — they mean it mathematically. If she got three, I should get three. If he got to stay up late, I should too. If they don't have homework, why do I?

This isn't brattiness. It's cognitive development. They're learning to compare, measure, and evaluate. Justice is being understood concretely before it can be understood abstractly.

If you have multiple children:

The fairness obsession intensifies with siblings. Every perceived inequality becomes evidence of favoritism. "You love her more" may become a refrain. Try to acknowledge the feeling without getting drawn into endless scorekeeping. "Fair" doesn't always mean "equal" — but that's a concept they're still building.

What helps:

- Take their social struggles seriously. The drama is real to them.
- Don't dismiss friendship problems as trivial.
- Help them name social dynamics without solving every problem for them.
- "Fair" doesn't mean "equal." Start introducing this — gently, repeatedly.
- Monitor but don't micromanage. They need to navigate some of this themselves.

The Rule Follower (and Rule Lawyer)

Something interesting happens with rules at this age: **they start to matter — intensely**.

The child who ignored your guidelines as a toddler may become almost rigid about rules as a 6 or 7-year-old. They want to know the rules. They want the rules applied consistently. And they will absolutely let you know when someone (including you) is breaking them.

This is healthy. Research shows that children this age are building their understanding of social order, fairness, and how systems work. Rules are how they make sense of the world.

But here's the flip side: they also become expert rule lawyers.

"You said I could have dessert if I finished dinner. I finished dinner. You didn't say I had to eat the vegetables."

"The rule is no screens before homework. I did my reading. Reading is homework. So technically..."

"You said 'in a minute.' It's been a minute."

This is exhausting. It's also a sign of developing logical thinking. They're testing the boundaries of language, consistency, and your patience — all at once.

What helps:

- Be precise with your language. They will find the loopholes.
- Acknowledge their logic, even when you're closing the loophole: "You're right, I wasn't specific. Let me be clear now."
- Model that rules can have exceptions without being invalid.
- Don't get into extended legal battles. State the intention, hold the line, move on.

Reading and the Inner World

If your child is reading now — really reading, for pleasure and meaning — something remarkable is happening:

They're developing an inner world you can't see.

Before literacy, their imaginative life was largely expressed outward — through play, through telling you, through drawing. Now, they can retreat into a book. They can have experiences you don't share. They can encounter ideas without you as intermediary.

This is the beginning of interiority — the private mental life that will define adolescence and adulthood.

Research shows this matters:

Children who read for pleasure develop stronger empathy, larger vocabularies, and better capacity for sustained attention. But beyond the measurable benefits, reading does something profound: it shows them that other minds exist, that perspectives differ, that their own inner experience is not the only one.

What this means for you:

- Protect reading time. It's not a luxury; it's development.
- Let them choose what they read (within reason). Engagement matters more than "level."
- Talk about books — not as quizzes, but as conversations. "What did you think about...?"
- Model reading yourself. They're still watching.

And notice: they're starting to have thoughts they don't share with you. This is normal and healthy. The seeds of privacy are being planted. Your job is to stay curious and available without demanding access to everything.

Fears Evolve

Remember the monster under the bed? The fear of the dark? The terror of the drain?

Those fears may be fading. But they're being replaced by something different — and in some ways, harder.

The fears of early childhood were imaginary. The fears of this age start to be real.

- Death — their own, yours, grandparents', pets'
- Disasters — fires, earthquakes, tornadoes, wars (especially if they see news)
- Rejection — being left out, not having friends, being embarrassed
- Failure — getting answers wrong, losing games, disappointing you
- The unknown — what happens next year? What if things change?

Research shows this shift is tied to cognitive development. They now understand enough about reality to know it contains genuine threats. But they don't yet have the emotional tools or life experience to put those threats in perspective.

What helps:

- Take fears seriously, even when they seem disproportionate.
- Provide honest, age-appropriate information. Don't lie, but don't overwhelm.
- Limit exposure to news and adult media. They hear more than you think.
- Reassure without dismissing: "It makes sense you're worried about that. Here's what I want you to know..."
- For death specifically: simple, honest, and repeated as needed. They'll ask again.

The Device Question: What Research Shows About Screens at This Age

You may be holding the line right now. No phone. Limited tablet time. Careful about what they watch.

And you may be feeling the pressure — from your child ("everyone else has one"), from other parents, from schools handing out Chromebooks, from your own exhaustion.

Here's what research suggests: **this is only the beginning, but it may be one of the most critical times to establish the patterns**.

What's happening in the brain at 5-7:

The brain's attention systems are actively developing during these years. Research shows that the capacity for *sustained attention* — the ability to focus on one thing for an extended period — is being wired right now.

Studies suggest that fast-paced screen content can interfere with this development. The rapid rewards and constant stimulation of screens train the brain to expect a level of stimulation that books, homework, and conversation simply can't match.

Boredom tolerance:

The capacity to tolerate boredom isn't a character trait — it's a skill that develops. Research indicates that children who have constant access to stimulation may struggle to develop this capacity. And boredom tolerance is linked to creativity, self-regulation, and resilience — skills they'll need for the rest of their lives.

When your child says "I'm bored," they're not reporting a problem you need to solve. They're experiencing discomfort that — if they learn to sit with it — becomes the birthplace of imagination, self-direction, and inner resourcefulness. Handing them a screen every time they're bored trains them to outsource that discomfort rather than develop the capacity to move through it.

Displacement:

Studies consistently show that the concern isn't just screen time itself — it's what screens replace. At this age, that's often unstructured play, face-to-face conversation, reading, and the kind of "productive boredom" that builds imagination.

The dopamine pattern:

Screens deliver rapid, unpredictable rewards — exactly what the dopamine system responds to most strongly. Research suggests this can create patterns that make slower, less stimulating activities (like reading, homework, or conversation) feel unbearable by comparison.

Why this age matters:

The habits formed now — around attention, boredom, and what we reach for when we're uncomfortable — become the defaults they carry into adolescence. And adolescence is when the stakes get much, much higher.

IT GETS HARDER AS THEY GET OLDER. The peer pressure intensifies.

The content gets darker. The dopamine loops get more sophisticated. The arguments get more persuasive. What you establish now is the foundation you'll stand on later.

WE'RE NOT TELLING YOU WHAT TO DO. Every family is different. But we are telling you: this is the time to be intentional. The decisions you make now — about devices, about limits, about your own screen use — are shaping neural pathways that will influence their capacity for attention, boredom tolerance, and self-regulation for years to come.

Different Architects, Different Timelines

Everything in this guide describes *typical* development. But you may have noticed that your child doesn't follow the typical map.

Maybe they're hitting some of these milestones early and others late. Maybe they process the world with unusual intensity — sensory, emotional, or both. Maybe they're brilliant at certain kinds of thinking and struggle with others. Maybe school is highlighting differences you'd only half-noticed before.

Here's what we want you to know:

Different isn't broken. Different is different.

Some children are wired to build their understanding of the world in non-typical ways. *Why Won't You Listen?* explores this in depth in its chapter on "Different Architects, Different Blueprints" — the idea that some brains are specialized builders, extraordinary at certain types of construction while following different timelines for others.

What this might look like at 5-7:

- A child who reads far above grade level but melts down over sock seams
- A child who can focus for hours on their passion but can't sit through a simple instruction
- A child who experiences every emotion at high volume
- A child who needs to move constantly in order to think
- A child who asks "what if" about everything — not anxiously, but systematically
- A child who seems years behind peers socially but years ahead intellectually (or vice versa)

What helps:

- **RESPECT THEIR BLUEPRINT.** They might build understanding in a different order, at a different pace, or with different materials. That's their architecture, not a flaw.

- **MORE REPETITIONS AREN'T FAILURE.** Where typical children need 10 repetitions, yours might need 100. That's thorough construction, not slow learning.

- **ADAPT, DON'T FORCE.** If they learn better while moving, let them move. If they need visual supports, provide them. If they can only process one thing at a time, respect that pace.

- **CELEBRATE UNUSUAL STRENGTHS.** The elaborate knowledge of dinosaurs or train schedules is still learning. It's practice. It's their brain doing what it does well.

If you're seeing persistent patterns that concern you — patterns that don't shift with patience and adaptation — trust your instincts and seek evaluation. Early support makes a significant difference, and getting help isn't labeling your child. It's understanding their blueprint so you can build with them, not against them.

What Your Child Needs

CONCRETE GUIDANCE. They're capable of logic, but they still need clear, specific expectations. "Be responsible" is too abstract. "Put your backpack by the door when you get home" is concrete.

CONSISTENT FOLLOW-THROUGH. They're testing whether the rules are real. If you say a consequence, follow through. If you make a promise, keep it. They're learning whether your words mean something.

ROOM TO QUESTION. They're going to ask "why" differently now — not with toddler curiosity, but with budding skepticism. This is healthy. Let them question (within limits). Explain your reasoning (briefly). Model that authority can be both firm and open.

HELP WITH THE SOCIAL WORLD. They can't navigate all of it alone. Listen to the drama. Help them name what's happening. Offer perspective without dismissing their experience.

HOMEWORK SUPPORT WITHOUT TAKEOVER. They need you nearby, available, helping them build systems. They don't need you doing it for them or turning every assignment into a battle.

PRESENCE DURING HARD THINGS. When they encounter death, failure, rejection, or fear — they need you close. Not to fix it. To help them bear it.

FREEDOM TO GROW. They need increasing independence — appropriate to your context and comfort level. Maybe that's walking to a neighbor's house; maybe it's choosing their own clothes or managing a small responsibility. The specifics vary by family and environment. The principle is the same: the leash is lengthening. Find ways to let it.

What It Looks Like When It's Working

- They can focus on a task for reasonable periods (not hours, but longer than before)
- They have friendships — even if they're sometimes rocky
- They can follow multi-step instructions
- They're curious about how things work
- They recover from disappointments (with time and support)
- They can articulate feelings, at least sometimes
- They push back on rules but ultimately comply with reasonable expectations
- They show empathy — not perfectly, but genuinely
- They have interests that are their own
- Connection with you is still strong, even as they need more independence

What's not on this list: perfect behavior, consistent logic, smooth emotional regulation, or easy compliance. They're still developing. Expect unevenness.

What It Looks Like When Support Is Needed

- Persistent difficulty making or keeping friends
- Extreme anxiety about school, performance, or separation
- Frequent, intense meltdowns that seem beyond typical frustration
- Inability to focus even briefly; constant restlessness
- Regression to earlier behaviors under stress
- Persistent sadness or withdrawal
- Significant struggles with reading or basic academics despite effort
- Excessive fears that interfere with daily life
- You feel consistently worried or disconnected

Trust your instincts. If something feels off, talk to their teacher, pediatrician, or a child psychologist. Early support makes a difference — and asking is not overreacting. Every child's timeline is different, but consistent struggles deserve attention.

Simple Connection Builders (5-7 Years)

ONE-ON-ONE TIME. Even 15 minutes of undivided attention matters. Let them choose the activity. Put your phone away. Be fully present.

BEDTIME CONVERSATIONS. This age often opens up at night, in the dark, when the day is settling. Lie with them for a few minutes. Ask open questions. Listen more than you talk.

GAMES WITH RULES. Board games, card games, simple sports — these build connection while teaching turn-taking, losing gracefully, and following rules. Play with them.

READ TOGETHER. Even if they can read independently, reading aloud together maintains connection. Chapter books with cliffhangers give you something to look forward to together.

SHARE YOUR OWN CHILDHOOD. They're old enough to hear age-appropriate stories about when you were their age. This builds connection and shows them you understand.

LET THEM TEACH YOU. Whatever they're into — Pokemon, gymnastics, dinosaurs — let them be the expert. Ask questions. Be genuinely curious. This validates their knowledge and reverses the usual dynamic.

PHYSICAL AFFECTION (IF THEY STILL WANT IT). Some kids this age start pulling away from hugs and cuddles. Follow their lead, but keep offering. A hand on the shoulder, a goodnight hug, a quick squeeze — connection doesn't require words.

REPAIR QUICKLY. When you lose your temper or handle something badly, come back and repair. "I got frustrated and raised my voice. That wasn't okay. I'm sorry." You're modeling accountability.

A Word for the Exhausted Parent

The exhaustion is different now.

You're not as physically depleted as you were with babies and toddlers. You're sleeping more. For many children this age, you can leave them in a room without constant supervision. (This varies, of course — you know your child and your environment. Some children need closer monitoring longer, and that's okay.)

But there's a new kind of tired:

The mental load of homework, schedules, activities, and social dynamics. The emotional labor of navigating their big feelings while managing your own. The vigilance of monitoring a world you can no longer fully control. The grief of watching them need you a little less each day.

And maybe, quietly, the worry: *Am I doing this right? Are they okay? Did I mess something up in those early years?*

Here's what the research says, and what we'll say again: **You don't have to be perfect. You have to be present.**

The relationship you've built is still the foundation. The connection you maintain through these years — through the homework battles and social dramas and screen negotiations and bedtime conversations — that's what carries them into adolescence and beyond.

They're watching how you handle stress. How you repair after conflict. How you treat people. How you manage your own screens, your own emotions, your own life.

You're still their primary model. That's exhausting. It's also an honor.

They won't remember every fight about homework. They'll remember whether you were there. Whether you listened. Whether they felt like they mattered to you.

You're doing that. Probably. Most of the time.

And that's enough.

The Mirror: Your Private Reflection

For your eyes only.

Your own experience of ages 5-7 is probably your first set of clear memories — school starting, friendships forming, the world expanding beyond your family.

What you experienced then shapes how you parent now, whether you realize it or not.

About Your Own Childhood (ages 5-7):

1. What do you remember about starting school?
    - Excitement and confidence
    - Anxiety and fear
    - A mix of both
    - Very little — it's hazy

2. How did your parents handle your academic performance?
    - Supportive regardless of outcomes
    - High expectations with pressure
    - Uninterested or uninvolved
    - Inconsistent – praise sometimes, criticism others
3. Did you have close friendships at this age?
    - Yes, and I felt secure socially
    - I struggled to make or keep friends
    - I was bullied or excluded
    - I don't remember clearly
4. When you were scared or worried, what happened?
    - My parents helped me feel safe
    - I was told not to worry or be silly
    - I learned to hide my fears
    - I don't remember
5. What do you wish your parents had understood about you at this age?

About Your Parenting Now:

6. When your child struggles academically or socially, your first reaction is:
    - Concern for their wellbeing
    - Anxiety about what it means
    - Frustration at the problem
    - A desire to fix it immediately

7. How do you handle their questions about hard topics (death, fairness, injustice)?
8. When they argue with your logic, how do you typically respond?
9. Is there a pattern from your own school years that you see repeating — or that you're working hard to avoid?
10. When do you feel most connected to your child now? Most disconnected?
11. What's one thing you're doing well that you want to keep doing?
12. What's one thing you want to do differently?

A Note on These Reflections

If these questions surfaced memories you haven't thought about in years — about school, about friendships, about how your parents handled your expanding world — that's the point.

We parent from our history, whether we know it or not. The scripts we absorbed at 6 and 7 are often the scripts we reach for when our own children are 6 and 7.

Some of those scripts serve us well. Others need rewriting.

You can keep what worked. You can change what didn't. But you can only do either if you see clearly what you're carrying.

That's what this reflection is for.

The Research Behind These Words

For clinicians, educators, researchers and those who want to verify the claims: full citations for claims made in each section follow. This book is designed to be recommended to clients and families as an accessible entry point to developmental research.

On the 5-to-7 shift: The concept of a fundamental cognitive reorganization between ages 5 and 7 has been recognized across developmental psychology (White, S.H., "Evidence for a Hierarchical Arrangement of Learning Processes," *Advances in Child Development and Behavior*, 2, 1965). Piaget identified this as the transition from preoperational to concrete operational thinking (Piaget, J., *The Psychology of Intelligence*, Routledge & Kegan Paul, 1950). Sheldon White's influential work documented this shift across multiple domains — cognitive, social, and behavioral (White, S.H., "The Child's Entry into the 'Age of Reason,'" in *The Five to Seven Year Shift: The Age of Reason and Responsibility*, University of Chicago Press, 1996). Cross-cultural research suggests this transition is recognized in societies worldwide, often marked by increased responsibilities and formal education (Rogoff, B., et al., "Age of Assignment of Roles and Responsibilities to Children: A Cross-Cultural Survey," *Human Development*, 18(5), 1975).

On brain development at this age: Research confirms that the brain reaches approximately 90-95% of its adult size by age 6-7 (Lenroot, R.K. & Giedd, J.N., "Brain Development in Children and Adolescents: Insights from Anatomical Magnetic Resonance Imaging," *Neuroscience & Biobehavioral Reviews*, 30(6), 2006). However, the prefrontal cortex — responsible for impulse control, planning, and executive function — continues developing into the mid-twenties (Casey, B.J., Giedd, J.N., & Thomas, K.M., "Structural and Functional Brain Development and Its Relation to Cognitive Development," *Biological Psychology*, 54(1-3), 2000). Studies using neuroimaging show significant changes in white matter organization and neural pruning during middle childhood, refining the brain's efficiency (Gogtay, N., et al., "Dynamic Mapping of Human Cortical Development During Childhood Through Early Adulthood," *Proceedings of the National Academy of Sciences*, 101(21), 2004).

On lying and cognitive development: Extensive research demonstrates that lying ability correlates with theory of mind development — the understanding that others have different knowledge and beliefs (Talwar, V. & Lee, K., "Social and Cognitive Correlates of Children's Lying Behavior," *Child Development*, 79(4), 2008). Studies show that almost all children lie by age 4, with sophistication increasing through middle childhood (Lee, K., "Little Liars: Development of Verbal Deception in Children," *Child Development Perspectives*, 7(2), 2013). Importantly, research shows that harsh punishment for lying tends to increase lying behavior, while environments emphasizing trust and safety reduce it (Talwar, V., et al., "Effects of a Punitive Environment on Children's Executive Functioning: A Natural Experiment," *Social Development*, 20(4), 2011; Talwar, V. & Lee, K., "A Punitive Environment Fosters Children's Dishonesty: A Natural Experiment," *Child Development*, 82(6), 2011).

On theory of mind: Research established that theory of mind — understanding that others have mental states different from one's own — develops significantly between ages 4-6 (Wellman, H.M., *Making Minds: How Theory of Mind Develops*, Oxford University Press, 2014). This cognitive achievement underlies social skills, empathy, deception, and communication. The classic "false belief" tasks demonstrate this development clearly (Wimmer, H. & Perner, J., "Beliefs About Beliefs: Representation and Constraining Function of Wrong Beliefs in Young Children's Understanding of Deception," *Cognition*, 13(1), 1983; Perner, J. & Lang, B., "Development of Theory of Mind and Executive Control," *Trends in Cognitive Sciences*, 3(9), 1999).

On homework effectiveness: Meta-analyses of homework research found that homework has minimal academic benefit for elementary school students (Cooper, H., Robinson, J.C., & Patall, E.A., "Does Homework Improve Academic Achievement? A Synthesis of Research, 1987-2003," *Review of Educational Research*, 76(1), 2006). The research suggests that for young children, the value of homework lies more in building habits and responsibility than in academic gains. Excessive homework or homework battles can actually harm attitudes toward learning (Cooper, H., *The Battle Over Homework: Common Ground for Administrators, Teachers, and Parents*, Corwin Press, 2007).

On screen time and attention development: Research found associations between early screen exposure and attention difficulties (Christakis, D.A., Zimmerman, F.J., DiGiuseppe, D.L., & McCarty, C.A., "Early Television Exposure and Subsequent Attentional Problems in Children," *Pediatrics*, 113(4), 2004). Studies suggest that fast-paced media may affect attention development (Lillard, A.S. & Peterson, J., "The Immediate Impact of Different

Types of Television on Young Children's Executive Function," *Pediatrics*, 128(4), 2011). The displacement hypothesis — that screen time's harm comes partly from replacing other activities — is supported by multiple studies (Radesky, J.S., Schumacher, J., & Zuckerman, B., "Mobile and Interactive Media Use by Young Children: The Good, the Bad, and the Unknown," *Pediatrics*, 135(1), 2015).

On reading and brain development: Research shows that learning to read creates new neural pathways and reorganizes brain architecture (Dehaene, S., *Reading in the Brain: The New Science of How We Read*, Penguin, 2009). Studies document that reading development during this period has lasting cognitive effects (Cunningham, A.E. & Stanovich, K.E., "Early Reading Acquisition and Its Relation to Reading Experience and Ability 10 Years Later," *Developmental Psychology*, 33(6), 1997). The transition from "learning to read" to "reading to learn" typically occurs during this age range.

On boredom and development: Research suggests that the capacity to tolerate boredom is a skill that develops, not an innate trait (Eastwood, J.D., Frischen, A., Fenske, M.J., & Smilek, D., "The Unengaged Mind: Defining Boredom in Terms of Attention," *Perspectives on Psychological Science*, 7(5), 2012). Studies link boredom tolerance to creativity, self-regulation, and resilience. Research on "constructive boredom" suggests that unstructured time without external stimulation supports imagination and self-directed activity (Gasper, K. & Middlewood, B.L., "Approaching Novel Thoughts: Understanding Why Elation and Boredom Promote Associative Thought More Than Distress and Relaxation," *Journal of Experimental Social Psychology*, 52, 2014).

On fear development: Research documents a predictable shift in children's fears between early and middle childhood (Gullone, E., "The Development of Normal Fear: A Century of Research," *Clinical Psychology Review*, 20(4), 2000). Younger children fear imaginary threats (monsters, the dark); older children increasingly fear realistic threats (death, injury, social rejection). This shift correlates with cognitive development — specifically, the growing understanding of real-world dangers (Muris, P., Merckelbach, H., Meesters, C., & van den Brand, K., "Cognitive Development and Worry in Normal Children," *Cognitive Therapy and Research*, 26(6), 2002; Ollendick, T.H., King, N.J., & Muris, P., "Fears and Phobias in Children: Phenomenology, Epidemiology, and Aetiology," *Child and Adolescent Mental Health*, 7(3), 2002).

On social development and peer relationships: Research documents the increasing importance of peer relationships in middle childhood (Rubin, K.H., Bukowski, W.M., & Parker, J.G., "Peer Interactions, Relationships, and Groups," in *Handbook of Child Psychology*, 6th ed., Wiley, 2006). Studies show that children this age engage in social comparison, develop awareness of social hierarchies, and form same-gender friendships predominantly (Hartup, W.W., "The Company They Keep: Friendships and Their Developmental Significance," *Child Development*, 67(1), 1996). Peer relationships at this age significantly influence social-emotional development (Parker, J.G. & Asher, S.R., "Peer Relations and Later Personal Adjustment: Are Low-Accepted Children at Risk?" *Psychological Bulletin*, 102(3), 1987).

On the "fairness" obsession: Piaget's work on moral development identified this age as characterized by a focus on rules, equality, and concrete justice (Piaget, J., *The Moral Judgment of the Child*, Free Press, 1932). Later research elaborated on how children's understanding of fairness evolves – from strict equality ("everyone gets the same") toward equity ("distribution based on need or merit") over time (Damon, W., *The Social World of the Child*, Jossey-Bass, 1977). Research shows that the concern with fairness at this age reflects genuine cognitive development, not mere selfishness (Fehr, E., Bernhard, H., & Rockenbach, B., "Egalitarianism in Young Children," *Nature*, 454(7208), 2008).

On fixed vs. growth mindset: Research documents that beliefs about intelligence significantly impact learning and persistence (Dweck, C.S., *Mindset: The New Psychology of Success*, Random House, 2006). Studies show that children praised for effort develop more resilient learning patterns than children praised for intelligence (Mueller, C.M. & Dweck, C.S., "Praise for Intelligence Can Undermine Children's Motivation and Performance," *Journal of Personality and Social Psychology*, 75(1), 1998). This effect is particularly relevant during the school transition years when children form academic identities.

On neurodivergent development: Research increasingly recognizes that developmental timelines vary significantly among children. Work on autism spectrum conditions, ADHD, sensory processing differences, and giftedness documents that many children follow non-typical developmental paths (Baron-Cohen, S., "The Extreme Male Brain Theory of Autism," *Trends in Cognitive Sciences*, 6(6), 2002; Barkley, R.A., *Attention-Deficit Hyperactivity Disorder: A Handbook for Diagnosis and Treatment*, 4th ed., Guilford Press, 2014). The neurodiversity paradigm frames these differences as variations rather than deficits (Armstrong, T., *Neurodiversity: Discovering the Extraordinary Gifts of Autism, ADHD, Dyslexia, and Other Brain Differences*, Da Capo Press, 2010).

On the logic trap: Research confirms that while logical reasoning emerges during this period, it remains concrete and situation-bound (Piaget, J. & Inhelder, B., *The Psychology of the Child*, Basic Books, 1969). Children can apply logic to tangible problems but struggle with abstract or hypothetical reasoning until adolescence. Studies show that parents often overestimate children's reasoning capacity based on their verbal abilities (Flavell, J.H., Miller, P.H., & Miller, S.A., *Cognitive Development*, 4th ed., Prentice Hall, 2002).

On the Tell, Show, Try, Do framework: Research supports the effectiveness of structured skill-teaching approaches that reduce cognitive load and provide safe opportunities for practice (Sweller, J., "Cognitive Load During Problem Solving: Effects on Learning," *Cognitive Science*, 12(2), 1988). Social learning theory documents the importance of modeling (Bandura, A., *Social Learning Theory*, Prentice Hall, 1977). Research on mastery vs. performance orientation shows that separating learning from evaluation improves outcomes (Dweck, C.S. & Leggett, E.L., "A Social-Cognitive Approach to Motivation and Personality," *Psychological Review*, 95(2), 1988).

BOOK FOUR:

The Forgotten Years

A Field Guide for Middle Childhood (7-12)

"The greatest gift we can give our children is to believe in them, even — especially — when they're not sure they believe in themselves ."

— Unknown

BOOK FOUR CONTENTS

A Note Before You Begin

Some of what follows may not describe your child today.

These years span a wide developmental range — a 7-year-old and an 11-year-old are in very different places. A child just entering middle childhood and one on the cusp of adolescence face different challenges, different pressures, different internal experiences.

This section serves two purposes: **understanding where your child is now, and preparing for where they're heading**.

Think of it as an owner's manual. When you buy a car, the manual tells you what the warning lights mean, what to do if something goes wrong, when to seek professional help. It's not predicting disaster — it's equipping you to respond if and when challenges arise.

That's what we're doing here.

If something doesn't apply to your child yet, file it away. You may need it sooner than you expect. And if you're fortunate enough to never need some of this information, you'll still be better equipped to support other families who do.

What's Actually Happening

Nobody writes books about this age.

Walk into any bookstore's parenting section and you'll find shelves devoted to babies, toddlers, and teenagers. But the years between 7 and 12? A handful of titles, if that. It's as if children disappear at seven and reappear at thirteen, fully formed adolescents ready to slam doors and roll eyes.

This is a mistake.

These are the forgotten years — and they may be among the most important of your child's development.

Here's what's actually happening:

Your child is consolidating. Everything they learned in the first seven years — attachment patterns, emotional regulation, communication skills, social understanding — is being integrated, practiced, and refined. They're building competence. Developing mastery. Forming an identity based on what they can do, who they're friends with, and where they fit.

Research calls this "middle childhood" or the "latency period." The drama of early childhood has calmed. The storm of adolescence hasn't arrived. It can feel like coasting.

It's not coasting. It's construction.

And around ages 9-11, something else begins: the brain starts preparing for its second major reorganization. The pre-adolescent changes that will explode into full adolescence are already beginning — quietly, beneath the surface.

These years are the bridge between the child they were and the teenager they're becoming. What happens on this bridge matters.

The Consolidation Years

Think of ages 7-12 as a builder completing a foundation before constructing the upper floors.

The foundation was poured in the early years — attachment, regulation, basic skills. Now your child is:

DEVELOPING COMPETENCE. They're getting genuinely good at things. Reading fluently. Doing real math. Playing instruments, sports, games with actual skill. This isn't just fun — it's identity formation. Research shows that children this age build self-concept largely through competence. "I'm someone who's good at soccer." "I'm a reader." "I'm the kid who knows about animals."

BUILDING INDUSTRY. Erikson called this stage "industry vs. inferiority." The developmental task is learning to work, to produce, to contribute. Children who develop a sense of industry feel capable and confident. Children who don't may carry feelings of inferiority into adolescence and beyond.

PRACTICING EVERYTHING. Social skills. Emotional regulation. Problem-solving. Conflict resolution. They're running drills on all the skills they'll need for the complexity of adolescence and adulthood. Every friendship negotiation, every homework completion, every managed disappointment is practice.

What this means for you:

These years might feel less urgent than the baby years, less demanding than the toddler years. You might finally feel like you can breathe.

Breathe — but stay engaged. The construction happening now is quieter but no less important. Your child is building the platform they'll stand on when adolescence hits.

The Social World Intensifies

If friendships mattered at 5-7, they become central at 7-12.

Your child's social world is now a full ecosystem — with hierarchies, alliances, unwritten rules, and consequences you may never fully see.

What research shows:

- Peer relationships become increasingly important across middle childhood
- Social comparison intensifies — they know exactly where they rank
- Cliques and groups form with clearer boundaries
- Bullying peaks during these years, particularly ages 10-12
- Social rejection is experienced as genuinely painful — brain imaging shows it activates the same regions as physical pain
- Same-gender friendships still dominate, but awareness of the other gender increases toward the end of this period

The hierarchy is real:

Your child knows who's popular and who's not. Who gets picked first and who gets picked last. Who has the right clothes, the right phone, the right whatever-matters-this-month.

This isn't superficiality. It's developmental. They're learning to read social systems, navigate group dynamics, and find their place. These are skills they'll use for the rest of their lives.

But it can also be brutal.

Bullying:

If bullying is going to happen, it often peaks in these years — particularly in late elementary and middle school. The social awareness is high enough to be weaponized, but the empathy and impulse control aren't fully developed.

Watch for:

- Reluctance to go to school
- Lost belongings, damaged items, unexplained injuries
- Changes in eating or sleeping
- Withdrawal from previously enjoyed activities
- Not wanting to talk about school or friends
- Declining grades

If you suspect bullying, take it seriously. Don't dismiss it as "kids being kids." Research shows that bullying has lasting effects on both victims and perpetrators. Involve the school. Document incidents. And keep communication with your child open — they need to know you're a safe place to land.

Peer pressure begins here:

It doesn't usually look like the after-school specials — kids explicitly pressuring your child to smoke behind the gym. It's subtler: the desire to fit in, to be liked, to not be different. The pressure isn't always spoken. It's felt.

Research shows that children with strong family relationships and clear internal values are more resistant to negative peer pressure. They still feel the pull — but they have something to weigh it against.

What helps:

- **TALK ABOUT INFLUENCE DIRECTLY.** "Who decides what's cool? How do you feel when everyone's doing something and you're not sure you want to?" Make the invisible visible.
- **ROLE-PLAY SCENARIOS.** "What would you do if your friends wanted to..." This isn't preachy — it's practice. Athletes practice before games. Kids can practice before pressure moments.
- **PRAISE INDEPENDENT THINKING.** When they make a choice that goes against the group, notice it. "That took courage."
- **HELP THEM FIND THEIR PEOPLE.** A child who has friends who share their values feels less pressure to conform to those who don't.

You can't remove peer influence — and you shouldn't try. Peers help children learn to navigate the social world. Your job is to make sure your influence remains alongside theirs, not replaced by it.

What helps with the social world overall:

- Take their social struggles seriously, even when they seem trivial
- Listen more than you advise
- Don't try to solve every problem — but stay informed
- Help them find at least one solid friendship; research shows even one good friend is protective
- Monitor without helicoptering — know who their friends are, where they spend time online

Teach them that social pain is real pain — validate their experiences

The Inner Life Deepens

Something shifts in these years: **you are no longer the center of their universe.**

This can hurt. The child who once told you everything now has secrets. The child who wanted to be with you constantly now closes their bedroom door. The child who thought you knew everything now corrects you (frequently).

This is healthy. This is supposed to happen.

The developmental task:

Children in middle childhood are developing what psychologists call "interiority" — a rich inner life that exists independently of you. They have thoughts they don't share. Feelings they process alone. Experiences you don't witness.

This is the foundation of privacy, autonomy, and ultimately, healthy adult identity.

What this looks like:

- Journals, diaries, notes marked "PRIVATE"
- Inside jokes with friends you don't understand

- Music, books, interests that are "theirs," not shared with you
- Less spontaneous sharing — you have to ask (and sometimes asking doesn't work)
- Opinions that differ from yours, sometimes just to differ
- A bedroom that becomes their territory

The access paradox:

When your child starts pulling away, the temptation is to pull harder. Demand access to their journal. Interrogate them about their day. Insist on knowing everything.

Research shows this often backfires.

Studies on "parental knowledge" — knowing where your child is, who they're with, what they're doing — confirm that this knowledge is protective. But the *source* of that knowledge matters enormously:

- **Child disclosure** (they tell you voluntarily) = best outcomes
- **Parental solicitation** (you ask and they answer) = moderate outcomes
- **Parental control/surveillance** (you demand or spy) = worst outcomes, often backfires

The more you demand access to your child's inner life, the less you often get. Children who feel surveilled become more secretive, not less. The goal is *voluntary disclosure* — creating conditions where they *want* to tell you things.

This means: staying curious without interrogating. Being available without hovering. Responding to what they share without overreacting (overreaction teaches them not to share next time). Asking open questions ("What was interesting today?") rather than closed ones ("Did anything bad happen?").

The balance:

Privacy doesn't mean absence. You still need to know where they are, who they're with, what they're doing online. But the information you most need — what's happening inside them — can only be given, not taken.

When they've really pulled away:

Sometimes the distance isn't just developmental. Sometimes a child withdraws in ways that feel like estrangement — refusing to talk, refusing connection, maybe even refusing to see you (particularly in divorced families).

This is painful. And the instinct is to push harder, demand connection, insist on relationship.

Research suggests that often makes it worse.

What helps:

- **STAY PRESENT WITHOUT PRESSURE.** Keep reaching out in low-key ways — a text, a note, a "thinking of you." Don't demand response.
- **OWN YOUR PART.** If you've made mistakes, acknowledge them specifically. Not endless apology — specific accountability. "I know I was too critical about school. I'm working on that."
- **DEMONSTRATE, DON'T JUST PROMISE.** Change has to be visible over time, not just declared.
- **GET SUPPORT.** A family therapist can sometimes bridge what direct communication can't.
- **BE PATIENT.** Repair takes longer than rupture. Keep the door open.

The relationship isn't necessarily over. But it may need time, space, and real change before it can be rebuilt.

The Pre-Adolescent Brain (9-12)

Around age 9 or 10 — sometimes earlier, sometimes later — something begins beneath the surface.

The brain is preparing for its second major reorganization.

What research shows:

Adolescence involves a massive restructuring of the brain — sometimes compared to the dramatic development of the first three years of life. But this restructuring doesn't wait for the teenage years to begin. The preliminary changes start in pre-adolescence:

- **GRAY MATTER PEAKS AND BEGINS TO PRUNE.** The brain overproduces neural connections, then begins eliminating the ones that aren't used. "Use it or lose it" becomes literal.
- **THE LIMBIC SYSTEM (EMOTIONAL BRAIN) BECOMES MORE ACTIVE.** Emotions may intensify before the prefrontal cortex catches up to regulate them.
- **HORMONAL CHANGES BEGIN.** Even before visible puberty, hormonal shifts are affecting mood, energy, and social behavior.

- **SLEEP PATTERNS START SHIFTING.** The circadian rhythm begins moving later — they're not just being difficult when they can't fall asleep at 8pm anymore.
- **RISK AWARENESS CHANGES.** The pre-adolescent brain is beginning to weigh risks differently, though the full risk-taking behavior of adolescence hasn't arrived.

The sleep shift:

Research shows that pre-adolescents genuinely need more sleep than they're often getting (9-12 hours), while their biology is pushing their sleep cycle later. Add screens (which suppress melatonin and stimulate the brain) and early school start times, and you have a recipe for chronic sleep deprivation.

Sleep deprivation in this age group is linked to mood problems, attention difficulties, academic struggles, and increased conflict. If your child seems irritable, unfocused, or emotionally volatile, consider whether they're getting enough sleep — and whether screens are interfering.

What this means:

Your 10-year-old may start showing flashes of the teenager to come:

- Moodiness that seems to come from nowhere
- Heightened emotional reactions
- Increased self-consciousness
- More interest in peers, less in family activities
- Testing boundaries in new ways
- Occasional eye-rolls, sighs, and "whatever"

This isn't failure. This isn't "early rebellion." This is biology. Their brain is beginning a process that will take over a decade to complete.

What helps:

- Know that this is normal — the preview of adolescence, not the full feature
- Stay calm when they're not calm
- Don't take the moodiness personally (easier said than done)
- Maintain routines and expectations even as they push against them
- Keep the relationship strong — you're building the bridge you'll need for adolescence
- Protect sleep — consistent bedtime, screens out of the bedroom, understanding that they may genuinely need a later bedtime as they approach adolescence

Screens: The Stakes Rise

Remember when we said "this is only the beginning" in the 5-7 section?

Welcome to the escalation.

The reality of 7-12:

- Many children get their first smartphone during these years
- Social media use often begins (despite age restrictions)
- Gaming becomes increasingly social and online
- Homework increasingly requires devices
- "Everyone has one" becomes a daily refrain
- The pressure — from peers, from kids themselves, sometimes from schools — is intense

What research shows:

The concerns we discussed earlier — attention, boredom tolerance, dopamine patterns — don't disappear. They compound. And new concerns emerge:

- **SOCIAL MEDIA AND MENTAL HEALTH.** Research increasingly links social media use in young adolescents to anxiety, depression, and negative body image — particularly for girls. The mechanisms include social comparison, cyberbullying, exposure to harmful content, and sleep disruption.
- **THE DISPLACEMENT PROBLEM GROWS.** At 5-7, screens displaced play and reading. At 7-12, they displace face-to-face social interaction during a critical period for social development. Research suggests that in-person social skills are built through practice — and screens reduce that practice.
- **THE DOPAMINE ESCALATION.** Games, social media, and video content are increasingly designed to be addictive. The dopamine hits become faster, more unpredictable, more compelling. The gap between screen stimulation and real-world stimulation widens.
- **THE CONTENT EXPOSURE PROBLEM.** Children this age may encounter pornography, violence, self-harm content, and extremist material — often accidentally. Research shows that early exposure to such content can have lasting effects.
- **THE ATTENTION FRAGMENTATION.** Studies suggest that heavy media multitasking in this age group correlates with reduced working memory and attention control. The brain is pruning during these years — and it's pruning based on what gets used.

The hard conversation:

We're not going to tell you whether or when to give your child a phone. Every family is different. Every child is different. Every community has different norms.

But we will tell you what the research suggests:

- **DELAY IS PROTECTIVE.** The longer you can delay smartphone and social media access, the more time their brain has to develop without those influences. Many researchers recommend waiting until at least age 14 for social media, and some recommend later.

- **YOU'RE NOT ALONE IF YOU HOLD THE LINE.** Organizations like Wait Until 8th (for smartphones) and movements for phone-free schools reflect growing awareness among parents and educators.
- **IF THEY HAVE A DEVICE, YOU NEED TO BE INVOLVED.** This isn't an age for "their privacy" to extend to unlimited, unmonitored internet access. Know what apps they're using. Have the devices charge outside their bedroom. Use parental controls — not as a perfect solution, but as one layer of protection.
- **YOUR OWN SCREEN USE MATTERS.** They're watching. If you can't put your phone down, your lectures about their phone use will ring hollow.

The "everyone has one" conversation:

They will tell you everyone has one. They may be largely right. Here are some responses:

- "I know it feels that way. This is a decision we've made for our family, and here's why..."
- "Some families make different choices. We're making this one."
- "You can be frustrated with this decision. I understand. The answer is still no for now."
- "Let's talk about what specifically you want to do, and whether there's another way to do it."

You will not win a popularity contest with this boundary. That's okay. You're not their friend. You're their parent. And protecting their developing brain from harms they can't fully understand is part of the job.

Homework, Academics, and Identity

School matters differently now.

In early elementary, school was about basics — learning to read, write, compute. In middle childhood, school becomes about identity.

What research shows:

- Academic self-concept solidifies during these years — "I'm smart" or "I'm not good at school" becomes baked in
- The transition to middle school (typically around ages 11-12) is a vulnerable period; many children experience a dip in engagement and achievement
- Homework has more academic value in these years than in early elementary — but excessive homework can still backfire
- Stress and anxiety related to school performance increase significantly

The identity risk:

Children who struggle academically in these years are at risk for internalizing "I'm not smart" as a core identity. This can affect motivation, effort, and willingness to try for years to come.

Watch for fixed mindset language: "I'm just not a math person." "I'm stupid." "I'll never get this."

Counter with growth mindset — not false praise, but accurate framing: "This is hard for you right now. Hard doesn't mean impossible. What would help?"

The overscheduling trap:

In an effort to give children every advantage, many families overschedule — sports, music, tutoring, clubs, activities filling every afternoon and weekend.

Research suggests this can backfire. Children need unstructured time for:

- Processing and integrating what they're learning
- Developing self-directed interests
- Rest and recovery
- Family connection
- Just being kids

A child who's exhausted, stressed, and constantly performing may look impressive on paper while struggling internally. Watch for signs: chronic tiredness, resistance to activities they used to enjoy, anxiety, or loss of the spontaneous joy that should still be present in childhood.

What helps:

- Stay involved without taking over — know what they're learning, what they're struggling with
- Help them develop systems — planners, routines, organizational strategies

- Focus on effort and strategy, not just outcomes
- Communicate with teachers early if you see problems
- Watch for signs of excessive stress or anxiety about performance
- Protect unstructured time — not every hour needs to be optimized for achievement
- Remember that grades aren't everything — character, curiosity, and connection matter too.

Chores and Contribution: Why Work Matters

This might seem old-fashioned. In an age of over-scheduled children and academic pressure, asking your child to take out the trash or fold laundry can feel like an unnecessary burden — or a battle not worth fighting.

The research says otherwise.

What studies show:

One of the longest-running studies in psychology — the Harvard Grant Study, which followed participants for over 75 years — found that childhood participation in household chores was one of the strongest predictors of professional success and life satisfaction in adulthood. Not grades. Not extracurriculars. Chores.

Why? Because chores teach things that can't be taught any other way:

- **RESPONSIBILITY.** Something needs to be done. You're the one who does it.
- **COMPETENCE.** You're capable of contributing, not just consuming.
- **DELAYED GRATIFICATION.** Work comes before play.

- **BELONGING.** You're a contributing member of this family, not a guest.
- **EXECUTIVE FUNCTION.** Planning, sequencing, completing — the same skills needed for school and work.

The modern trap:

Many parents today skip chores — out of guilt, out of time pressure, out of the belief that childhood should be carefree, or simply because it's easier to do it themselves.

Research suggests this is a mistake. Children who contribute to the household don't just become more capable adults — they're often happier *now*. Contribution builds self-worth. Being needed feels good.

What this looks like at 7-12:

- **7-8:** Making bed, setting/clearing table, feeding pets, putting away laundry, tidying room, helping with simple meal prep
- **9-10:** Vacuuming, loading dishwasher, taking out trash, packing own lunch, caring for pets independently, helping with younger siblings
- **11-12:** Cooking simple meals, doing own laundry, cleaning bathrooms, yard work, managing own space and belongings, contributing to family projects

How to make it work:

- **MAKE IT NON-NEGOTIABLE.** Chores are part of family membership, not optional extras.
- **BE CONSISTENT.** Same expectations, same time, same follow-through.
- **DON'T REDO THEIR WORK IN FRONT OF THEM.** Good enough is good enough. Perfectionism kills motivation.

- **WORK ALONGSIDE THEM WHEN POSSIBLE.** Especially at first. This builds skill and connection.
- **SEPARATE CHORES FROM ALLOWANCE.** Chores are contribution. Allowance (if you give it) is for learning money management. Conflating them teaches that you only work when paid.
- **EXPECT RESISTANCE.** Do it anyway. They don't have to like it. They have to do it.

You're not burdening your child by asking them to contribute. You're preparing them for a life where effort is required and contribution matters. That's a gift — even if they don't see it that way yet.

Teaching new tasks: Tell, Show, Try, Do

When children refuse chores or do them poorly, parents often assume the worst — laziness, defiance, disrespect.

But research suggests that sloppy work or outright refusal often has a simpler cause: **a step was skipped in the teaching process**.

A framework that works across ages and tasks:

TELL. Give clear, complete instruction. "Do the laundry" is too vague for someone who's never done it. "Sort colors and whites, use this much detergent, set it to this cycle, move it to the dryer when it beeps, fold it when it's done" is instruction.

SHOW. Do the entire task while they observe. No participation yet — just watching. This accomplishes two things: it proves the task is possible (removing "I can't"), and it creates a mental picture of what "done" looks like.

TRY. Their turn. You watch. This is the critical step — and the one most often botched. Don't correct them mid-task. Don't take over when they're slow. Don't sigh or show frustration. Let them struggle. Let them finish. Questions are welcome. Rescue is not.

DO. Now it's theirs. Practice builds competence. Ownership builds pride. *Encourage them to find a better way.* When they discover an efficiency you didn't teach them, that's the goal — they've made it their own.

Why this works:

Each stage removes a barrier:

- **TELL** removes uncertainty ("What am I supposed to do?")
- **SHOW** removes doubt ("Is this even possible?")
- **TRY** removes fear of failure ("What if I mess up?")
- **DO** removes external ownership ("This is my task now")

When things go wrong:

If your child refuses a task → check whether SHOW happened. They may not believe they can do it.

If they do it poorly → check whether TRY was ever safe. If early attempts were criticized, they may be failing on purpose (conscious or not) to avoid the pressure of trying.

If they have no pride in the work → check whether DO was ever given. If you redo their work or micromanage their method, they never owned it.

The framework isn't just about chores. It applies to any skill you want to transfer: homework routines, money management, cooking, time management. Tell. Show. Try. Do. Then step back and let them own it.

The Body Starts Changing

For some children, puberty begins during these years. For others, it's approaching. For all of them, awareness of bodies — their own and others' — increases.

The wide range of normal:

Puberty can begin as early as 8 in girls and 9 in boys, or as late as 13 or 14. This means a 10-year-old classroom might contain children who look like young adults alongside children who still look like children.

This variation is normal — but it doesn't feel normal to the kids experiencing it. The early bloomer feels like a freak. The late bloomer feels left behind. Everyone is comparing.

What helps:

- Provide accurate, age-appropriate information before they need it — don't wait until they ask
- Normalize the variation: "Bodies develop at different rates. There's no right time."
- Books can help start conversations — there are excellent resources for this age

- Keep the door open: "If you ever have questions about your body or growing up, I'm here."
- Watch for signs that body changes are causing distress
- For girls especially: the cultural messages about bodies are brutal. Counter them.

Identity questions:

For some children, these years bring early questions about identity — including gender and sexuality. They may not have answers, and they may not share their questions with you. But they're increasingly aware that such questions exist.

If your child does share questions or confusion about identity, your response in this moment matters more than you know. You don't have to have all the answers. But responding with curiosity and love rather than panic or dismissal keeps the door open for ongoing conversation.

What helps: "Thank you for telling me. I'm glad you trust me with this. Let's talk about what you're experiencing." What doesn't help: "You're too young to know that" or "That's just a phase" or immediate alarm.

The conversation about consent and bodies:

This is also the age to reinforce body autonomy and consent — their right to say no to unwanted touch, the importance of respecting others' boundaries, and the basics of what healthy relationships look like.

These conversations lay groundwork for adolescence. Better to have them now, in the calm, than later, in the storm.

A Word About Divorce

If you're going through a divorce, or have been through one, you may be carrying guilt about how it's affecting your child.

Here's what research actually shows: divorce itself isn't what harms children most. What harms them is ongoing conflict between parents, loss of relationship with one parent, and being caught in the middle.

Children of divorce do well when:

- Both parents stay involved and cooperative
- The child isn't used as messenger, spy, or confidant
- Neither parent bad-mouths the other (even when it's deserved)
- Routines and stability are maintained where possible
- The child has explicit permission to love both parents

You can't control the other parent. You can control whether you put your child in the middle. You can control whether you speak ill of their other parent in front of them. You can control whether you fight through them or around them.

Your child doesn't need a perfect family. They need parents who can manage their own pain without making the child carry it.

If your child is struggling with the divorce — changes in behavior, withdrawal, anger, anxiety — consider family therapy or individual therapy for them. Divorce is a loss, and losses need to be grieved. Professional support can help.

When Harder Things Happen

Most children navigate middle childhood without major crisis. But some encounter significant struggles during these years. Being prepared helps you respond rather than react.

Grief and loss:

Death often enters a child's life during these years — grandparents, pets, sometimes friends or family members. They understand death differently now than they did at younger ages. It's real, permanent, and frightening.

What helps:

- Honest, age-appropriate information
- Permission to grieve in their own way (which may not look like adult grief)
- Maintaining routines where possible
- Your own willingness to acknowledge the loss and share your feelings
- Patience — grief doesn't follow a timeline

If a death significantly disrupts their functioning for more than a few months, or if they express hopelessness about their own life, seek professional support.

Early substance exposure:

For some children, ages 10-12 bring first exposure to alcohol, vaping, or other substances — through peers, older siblings, or media. They may not be using, but they're aware.

This is a time for conversation, not just prohibition. Research shows that children who understand *why* substances are harmful (especially to developing brains) and who can talk openly with parents are more resistant to early use.

What helps:

- Start conversations before you think you need to
- Be clear about your expectations and the reasons behind them
- Ask what they're seeing and hearing
- Make it safe to tell you things without explosion
- Know their friends and, when possible, their friends' parents

Anxiety:

Anxiety in children often peaks during these years, particularly around ages 10-12 as social and academic pressures increase and the pre-adolescent brain changes begin.

Signs to watch for:

- Excessive worry about school, friends, family, health, or the future
- Physical complaints (stomachaches, headaches) especially before school or social events
- Avoidance of activities they used to enjoy
- Difficulty sleeping

- Need for constant reassurance
- Perfectionism that causes distress

Anxiety is highly treatable, especially when caught early. If you're seeing persistent patterns, talk to your pediatrician or a child psychologist.

Depression:

Depression in children is real — and it often looks different than adult depression.

In children, depression may show up as:

- Irritability more than sadness
- Physical complaints without medical cause
- Declining academic performance
- Social withdrawal
- Changes in sleep or appetite
- Loss of interest in previously enjoyed activities
- Negative self-talk ("I'm worthless," "Nobody likes me," "Nothing matters")
- Hopelessness about the future

Research shows that childhood depression is increasing — and that it's often missed because we don't expect it in children this young.

If you're seeing these patterns persistently (more than two weeks), don't wait. Talk to your pediatrician or a mental health professional. Childhood depression responds well to treatment — but untreated, it can deepen and persist.

Self-harm:

In recent years, self-harm (cutting, burning, hitting oneself) has appeared in younger children — sometimes as young as 8 or 9, more commonly starting around 10-12.

Signs to watch for: unexplained cuts, burns, or bruises; wearing long sleeves in warm weather; reluctance to change clothes in front of others; isolation after emotional incidents.

If you see these signs, take them seriously. Always.

Self-harm requires professional support — not punishment, not panic, but real help. Approach with concern, not accusation: "I noticed some marks on your arm. I'm not angry — I'm worried. I need to understand what's happening so I can help."

Don't try to assess the risk yourself. Contact your pediatrician or a mental health professional immediately. If your child expresses thoughts of suicide or you're concerned about immediate safety, call 988 (Suicide and Crisis Lifeline) or go to your nearest emergency room.

Your calm, non-judgmental response matters — but so does getting professional help quickly.

Staying Connected: Especially When Time Is Short

Maybe you're a single parent juggling everything. Maybe both parents work long hours. Maybe life is just relentless right now.

Research offers some relief: connection is about quality and consistency, not quantity. Five minutes of full presence — phone down, eyes on them, fully there — matters more than an hour of distracted proximity.

What works when time is short:

PROTECT THE TRANSITIONS. How you greet them when they come home and how you say goodnight are high-value moments. Make them count. Put the phone down. Make eye contact. Touch them. Show them they matter.

RITUALIZE SOMETHING SMALL. Saturday morning breakfast. A weekly walk. Ten minutes before bed. Small rituals maintained over time build connection. They become anchors in the chaos.

USE CAR TIME. You're already driving them places. Make it screen-free (for both of you). Let conversation happen. Don't interrogate — just be present. Some of the best conversations happen when you're not looking at each other.

EAT TOGETHER WHEN YOU CAN. Research consistently links family meals to positive outcomes — better grades, lower substance use, better mental health. It doesn't have to be every night. But protect what you can.

BE PREDICTABLE. When time is limited, predictability creates security. They know when they'll have you, even if it's not as much as either of you wishes.

ONE-ON-ONE TIME. Even monthly, even briefly. Each child getting some undivided attention makes a measurable difference.

BE PRESENT WHEN YOU'RE PRESENT. The time you do have matters most if you're actually there — not scrolling, not distracted, not half-listening while you think about work. Quality requires presence.

You don't have to be present all the time. You have to be *fully* present *some* of the time. For children, that's enough to maintain connection.

The Bridge to Adolescence

These years are a bridge.

On one side: the child they were, who needed you for everything, who saw you as all-knowing, who lived primarily in your world.

On the other side: the teenager they're becoming, who needs you differently, who will question everything you say, who will build their own world — sometimes in opposition to yours.

What you're building now:

- **THE RELATIONSHIP THAT WILL CARRY YOU THROUGH ADOLESCENCE.** Research consistently shows that the parent-child relationship in middle childhood predicts outcomes in adolescence. Stay connected now, and you have something to draw on later.
- **THE COMMUNICATION PATTERNS THAT WILL MATTER WHEN IT COUNTS.** If you can talk about the small stuff now, you're more likely to hear about the big stuff later.
- **THE TRUST THAT ALLOWS APPROPRIATE INDEPENDENCE.** A teenager who was never trusted with small freedoms will either be unprepared for independence or will take it without your blessing.

- **THE VALUES THEY'LL CARRY FORWARD.** They're watching everything — how you treat people, what you prioritize, how you handle difficulty. These years are your last extended opportunity to model before they become more peer-influenced.

What's coming:

Adolescence is not a disease. It's a profound developmental process — arguably the most significant reorganization of the brain since the first years of life.

Your teenager will need to:

- Separate from you enough to become their own person
- Take risks in order to learn about the world
- Form an identity independent of the one you gave them
- Orient increasingly toward peers and toward the future they're building

This is supposed to happen. It's how humans develop into adults.

Your job in these final years of childhood is not to prevent adolescence. It's to prepare for it — to build a relationship strong enough to survive the turbulence, to equip your child with the skills they'll need, and to begin letting go so they can begin taking hold.

If your child is already in the thick of this — anxious, overwhelmed, drowning in comparison — they may need something written for them, not about them. Recognition Press is developing resources that speak directly to this generation in their language, without the self-help pressure. Sometimes the best thing a parent can do is point their child toward words that say what you can't. Visit recognitionpress.com for upcoming releases.

What Your Child Needs

CONTINUED CONNECTION. They may act like they don't need you. They do. Find ways to stay connected that respect their growing independence — side-by-side activities, car rides, low-pressure time together.

INCREASING AUTONOMY. They need practice making decisions, managing time, handling money, navigating social situations. Let them. Let them fail small so they can succeed big later.

YOUR CALM PRESENCE WHEN THINGS GO WRONG. Friendship drama. Academic failure. Embarrassment. Rejection. These are coming. They need you to be the steady presence, not the panicked responder.

RESPECT FOR THEIR INNER LIFE. They're becoming their own person. Let them. Don't demand access to every thought.

CLEAR EXPECTATIONS AND CONSISTENT FOLLOW-THROUGH. They'll push against limits. They still need them. Be firm and kind.

MONITORING WITHOUT SURVEILLANCE. Know where they are, who they're with, what they're doing online. But don't read their diary.

REAL RESPONSIBILITY. Chores, contribution, meaningful work. They need to be needed.

PREPARATION, NOT PROTECTION. You can't protect them from adolescence. You can prepare them for it. Teach them. Equip them.

Trust them.

What It Looks Like When It's Working

- They have at least one solid friendship
- They have interests and activities that bring them satisfaction
- They can manage schoolwork with reasonable support
- They recover from setbacks (with time)
- They still talk to you, even if not about everything
- They show increasing responsibility and independence
- They have their own opinions — even ones you disagree with
- They still seek you out sometimes — for comfort, advice, or just presence
- They contribute to the household
- They're growing into a person you're starting to see glimpses of

What's not on this list: perfect grades, constant happiness, zero conflict, or unchanged closeness. They're developing. Expect evolution.

What It Looks Like When Support Is Needed

- Persistent social isolation or lack of any friendships
- Bullying — as victim or perpetrator
- Significant and sustained drop in academic performance
- Signs of depression: persistent irritability or sadness, withdrawal, loss of interest
- Signs of anxiety: excessive worry, physical complaints, avoidance
- Signs of self-harm: unexplained marks, wearing concealing clothing, isolation
- Disordered eating or excessive concern with weight/body
- Talk of self-harm, suicide, or hopelessness
- Significant behavior changes without clear cause
- Excessive screen use that's affecting sleep, relationships, or functioning
- You feel consistently worried or disconnected

Trust your instincts. If something feels wrong, it might be. Talk to their doctor, school counselor, or a mental health professional. Early intervention matters.

Crisis resources:

- 988 — Suicide and Crisis Lifeline (call or text)
- Crisis Text Line — Text HOME to 741741
- Your nearest emergency room for immediate safety concerns.

Simple Connection Builders (7–12)

FIND THEIR THING. Whatever they're into — gaming, sports, music, art, animals, coding — take genuine interest. Let them teach you. Show up for their events.

CAR TIME. Something about facing forward instead of face-to-face opens kids up. Don't interrogate. Just be present. Let conversation happen.

ONE-ON-ONE TIME. Even 15 minutes of undivided attention matters, especially in families with multiple children. Make it regular.

MEALS TOGETHER. Research consistently links family meals to positive outcomes in adolescence. Protect this time.

KEEP BEDTIME RITUALS. They may be "too old" for stories, but a few minutes of quiet connection before sleep still matters.

PHYSICAL AFFECTION. If they still want it, keep giving it. If they've pulled away, respect it — but keep offering small gestures. A hand on the shoulder. A quick hug. Touch matters.

SHARE YOUR OWN STORIES. They're old enough for more of your history now. Age-appropriate stories about your own middle school years, your struggles, your mistakes. This normalizes their experience and builds connection.

WORK ALONGSIDE THEM. Chores, projects, cooking — side-by-side activity creates natural opportunities for conversation.

ADMIT WHEN YOU'RE WRONG. Model accountability. "I overreacted. I'm sorry. Let me try again."

A Word for the Exhausted Parent

You made it through the baby years. The toddler years. The endless questions and the homework battles and the friendship drama and the screen negotiations.

And now, just when you thought you could breathe, you're watching the preview of adolescence — the moodiness, the eye-rolls, the closed doors.

Here's what you might need to hear:

You still matter.

Research is clear on this: parents remain the most significant influence on children through adolescence and into adulthood — even when it doesn't feel like it. Even when they act like you're irrelevant. Even when they quote their friends like scripture and dismiss everything you say.

You still matter. The relationship you're building now still matters. The values you're modeling still matter. The safety you provide still matters.

The distance is necessary.

They're supposed to pull away. They're supposed to develop their own inner life, their own opinions, their own world. This isn't rejection of you — it's development of them.

Let them go a little. Keep the connection strong while the distance grows. Both things are possible. Both things are necessary.

The storm is coming.

Adolescence will bring new challenges. But you'll face them with years of relationship behind you. You'll face them with a child who's been practicing regulation, social skills, and communication. You'll face them with whatever trust and connection you've built in these forgotten years.

That's your foundation for what comes next.

You've done more than you know.

The thousands of small moments — the conversations, the car rides, the homework help, the bedtime rituals, the repairs after conflict — they add up. They're wired in. They're part of who your child is becoming.

You can't see the architecture you've built. But it's there.

They won't remember most of it specifically. But they'll carry it. And when adolescence hits, when adulthood comes, when they become parents themselves — they'll have what you gave them.

You've got this. Probably. Most of the time.

And that's always been enough.

The Mirror: Your Private Reflection

For your eyes only.

Your experience of middle childhood — ages 7-12 — shaped you in ways you may not fully recognize. These were the years of school, friendships, activities, identity formation. What happened then is still with you now.

About Your Own Middle Childhood:

1. What do you remember about your friendships at this age?
    - I felt secure and connected
    - I struggled to fit in
    - I was bullied or excluded
    - I was part of the "in" crowd
    - I had one close friend and that was enough

2. How did your parents handle your growing independence?
    - They gave me appropriate freedom
    - They were too controlling
    - They were too absent
    - It varied — sometimes too much, sometimes too little
3. What was school like for you?
    - A place of success and confidence
    - A place of struggle and stress
    - Socially hard, academically fine
    - Academically hard, socially fine
    - Somewhere I just tried to survive
4. Did you feel like your parents "got" you at this age?
5. What do you wish they had understood?

About Your Parenting Now:

6. When your child pulls away or wants privacy, your gut reaction is:
    - Respect for their development
    - Anxiety about what they're hiding
    - Hurt or rejection
    - Relief that they're becoming independent
7. How do you handle their social world — the friendships, the drama, the hierarchy?
8. What's your biggest worry for them in these years?
9. Is there a pattern from your own middle childhood that you see repeating — or that you're working hard to avoid?
10. What do you want them to remember about these years, looking back?
11. What's one thing you're doing well that you want to keep doing?
12. What's one thing you want to do differently?

A Note on These Reflections

Your middle childhood probably shaped your sense of identity, your social confidence, your relationship with achievement, and your understanding of where you fit.

Some of that may be worth keeping. Some may be worth changing.

The beauty of parenting is that you get to keep what worked and build something new where it didn't. Your child isn't you. Their middle childhood doesn't have to be yours.

But you have to see what you're carrying before you can choose what to pass on.

That's what this reflection is for.

The Research Behind These Words

For clinicians, educators, researchers and those who want to verify the claims: full citations for claims made in each section follow. This book is designed to be recommended to clients and families as an accessible entry point to developmental research.

On middle childhood as a developmental stage: Erikson identified the key developmental task of this period as "industry vs. inferiority" — developing a sense of competence and capability (Erikson, E.H., *Childhood and Society*, W.W. Norton, 1950). Research confirms that self-concept and academic identity solidify during these years, with lasting effects on motivation and achievement (Eccles, J.S., "The Development of Children Ages 6 to 14," *The Future of Children*, 9(2), 1999). Middle childhood is sometimes called the "forgotten years" because it receives less research attention than early childhood or adolescence, despite its developmental significance (Collins, W.A., ed., *Development During Middle Childhood: The Years from Six to Twelve*, National Academy Press, 1984).

On the pre-adolescent brain: Neuroimaging studies document significant brain changes beginning around ages 9-11, including gray matter pruning, increased limbic system activity, and early hormonal changes (Giedd, J.N., et al., "Brain Development During Childhood and Adolescence: A Longitudinal MRI Study," *Nature Neuroscience*, 2(10), 1999). Research has mapped these developmental trajectories using longitudinal brain imaging (Lenroot, R.K. & Giedd, J.N., "Brain Development in Children and Adolescents: Insights from Anatomical Magnetic Resonance Imaging," *Neuroscience & Biobehavioral Reviews*, 30(6), 2006). The emotional intensity often seen in pre-adolescents reflects limbic system development outpacing prefrontal cortex maturation (Casey, B.J., Jones, R.M., & Hare, T.A., "The Adolescent Brain," *Annals of the New York Academy of Sciences*, 1124(1), 2008).

On peer relationships in middle childhood: Research documents the increasing importance of peer relationships across this period (Rubin, K.H., Bukowski, W.M., & Parker, J.G., "Peer Interactions, Relationships, and Groups," in *Handbook of Child Psychology*, 6th ed., Wiley, 2006). Studies show that social rejection activates the same brain regions as physical pain (Eisenberger, N.I., Lieberman, M.D., & Williams, K.D., "Does Rejection Hurt? An fMRI Study of Social Exclusion," *Science*, 302(5643), 2003). Peer victimization has lasting effects on mental health (Reijntjes, A., Kamphuis, J.H., Prinzie, P., & Telch, M.J., "Peer Victimization and Internalizing Problems in Children: A Meta-Analysis of Longitudinal Studies," *Child Abuse & Neglect*, 34(4), 2010).

On bullying: Research indicates that bullying peaks in late elementary and middle school years (Nansel, T.R., et al., "Bullying Behaviors Among U.S. Youth: Prevalence and Association with Psychosocial Adjustment," *JAMA*, 285(16), 2001). Meta-analyses show significant negative effects for both victims and perpetrators (Ttofi, M.M. & Farrington, D.P., "Effectiveness of School-Based Programs to Reduce Bullying: A Systematic and Meta-Analytic Review," *Journal of Experimental Criminology*, 7(1), 2011). Interventions are most effective when they involve the whole school community rather than just individuals (Olweus, D., *Bullying at School: What We Know and What We Can Do*, Blackwell, 1993).

On parental knowledge and monitoring: Research distinguishes between child disclosure, parental solicitation, and parental control as sources of parental knowledge (Stattin, H. & Kerr, M., "Parental Monitoring: A Reinterpretation," *Child Development*, 71(4), 2000). Studies show that child disclosure is associated with the best outcomes, while surveillance and control often backfire (Kerr, M. & Stattin, H., "What Parents Know, How They Know It, and Several Forms of Adolescent Adjustment: Further Support for a Reinterpretation of Monitoring," *Developmental Psychology*, 36(3), 2000). Creating conditions that promote voluntary disclosure is more effective than demanding information (Soenens, B., Vansteenkiste, M., Luyckx, K., & Goossens, L., "Parenting and Adolescent Problem Behavior: An Integrated Model with Adolescent Self-Disclosure and Perceived Parental Knowledge as Intervening Variables," *Developmental Psychology*, 42(2), 2006).

On screen time and adolescent mental health: The research in this area is moving fast, and it's being contested. Some researchers argue the effects are overstated; others believe they're understated. What isn't contested: the design is intentional. B.J. Fogg's Persuasive Technology Lab at Stanford trained many of the designers who built these platforms. Nir Eyal literally wrote a book called "Hooked: How to Build Habit-Forming Products." Former Google design ethicist Tristan Harris has testified before Congress about manipulation techniques. The question isn't whether your child's attention is being engineered — it's how much that engineering affects them specifically. Research has documented correlations between social media use and mental health difficulties in adolescents, particularly girls

(Twenge, J.M., Joiner, T.E., Rogers, M.L., & Martin, G.N., "Increases in Depressive Symptoms, Suicide-Related Outcomes, and Suicide Rates Among U.S. Adolescents After 2010 and Links to Increased New Media Screen Time," *Clinical Psychological Science*, 6(1), 2018). While causation remains debated, multiple studies support the association (Haidt, J. & Allen, N., "Scrutinizing the Effects of Digital Technology on Mental Health," *Nature*, 578(7794), 2020). Mechanisms including social comparison, sleep disruption, and displacement of in-person interaction have been proposed (Primack, B.A., et al., "Social Media Use and Perceived Social Isolation Among Young Adults in the U.S.," *American Journal of Preventive Medicine*, 53(1), 2017).

On family meals: Research consistently links regular family meals to positive outcomes including better academic performance, lower rates of substance use, and better mental health in adolescence (Fulkerson, J.A., Story, M., Mellin, A., Leffert, N., Neumark-Sztainer, D., & French, S.A., "Family Dinner Meal Frequency and Adolescent Development: Relationships with Developmental Assets and High-Risk Behaviors," *Journal of Adolescent Health*, 39(3), 2006). The mechanism appears to involve both connection and communication (Fiese, B.H., Foley, K.P., & Spagnola, M., "Routine and Ritual Elements in Family Mealtimes: Contexts for Child Well-Being and Family Identity," *New Directions for Child and Adolescent Development*, 2006(111), 2006).

On chores and development: The Harvard Grant Study, one of the longest longitudinal studies in psychology, found that participation in household chores during childhood was among the strongest predictors of professional success and life satisfaction in adulthood (Vaillant, G.E., *Triumphs of Experience: The Men of the Harvard Grant Study*, Belknap Press, 2012). Additional research links chores to the development of responsibility, executive function, and sense of belonging (Rende, R. & Prosek, J., *Raising Can-Do Kids: Giving Children the Tools to Thrive in a Fast-Changing World*, Perigee, 2015; White, E.M., DeBoer, M.D., & Scharf, R.J., "Associations Between Household Chores and Childhood Self-Competency," *Journal of Developmental & Behavioral Pediatrics*, 40(3), 2019).

On parent influence through adolescence: Contrary to popular belief, research shows that parents remain the most significant influence on children through adolescence (Steinberg, L., *Age of Opportunity: Lessons from the New Science of Adolescence*, Houghton Mifflin Harcourt, 2014). While peer influence increases, parental influence doesn't disappear — particularly regarding values, long-term decisions, and sense of security (Collins, W.A., Maccoby, E.E., Steinberg, L., Hetherington, E.M., & Bornstein, M.H., "Contemporary Research on Parenting: The Case for Nature and Nurture," *American Psychologist*, 55(2), 2000).

On puberty timing: Research documents wide variation in pubertal timing and shows that both early and late development can be challenging (Mendle, J., Turkheimer, E., & Emery, R.E., "Detrimental Psychological Outcomes Associated with Early Pubertal Timing in Adolescent Girls," *Developmental Review*, 27(2), 2007). Early-maturing girls face particular risks including earlier sexual activity and higher rates of depression (Graber, J.A., "Pubertal

Timing and the Development of Psychopathology in Adolescence and Beyond," *Hormones and Behavior*, 64(2), 2013). Supporting children through pubertal variation with accurate information and emotional availability is protective (Dorn, L.D. & Biro, F.M., "Puberty and Its Measurement: A Decade in Review," *Journal of Research on Adolescence*, 21(1), 2011).

On academic self-concept: Research in educational psychology shows that academic self-concept solidifies during middle childhood and strongly predicts later achievement and motivation (Marsh, H.W. & Martin, A.J., "Academic Self-Concept and Academic Achievement: Relations and Causal Ordering," *British Journal of Educational Psychology*, 81(1), 2011). Dweck's work on growth mindset documents the importance of how children understand their own abilities (Dweck, C.S., *Mindset: The New Psychology of Success*, Random House, 2006). Fixed mindset beliefs that emerge during this period can have lasting effects on academic engagement (Blackwell, L.S., Trzesniewski, K.H., & Dweck, C.S., "Implicit Theories of Intelligence Predict Achievement Across an Adolescent Transition: A Longitudinal Study and an Intervention," *Child Development*, 78(1), 2007).

On middle school transition: Research consistently shows that the transition to middle school is associated with declines in academic motivation and achievement for many students (Eccles, J.S., Wigfield, A., Midgley, C., Reuman, D., Iver, D.M., & Feldlaufer, H., "Negative Effects of Traditional Middle Schools on Students' Motivation," *Elementary School Journal*, 93(5), 1993). Factors include changes in school structure, increased academic demands, and social reorganization (Simmons, R.G. & Blyth, D.A., *Moving into Adolescence: The Impact of Pubertal Change and School Context*, Aldine de Gruyter, 1987).

On childhood anxiety and depression: Research documents increasing rates of anxiety and depression in children, with onset often occurring in middle childhood (Merikangas, K.R., et al., "Lifetime Prevalence of Mental Disorders in U.S. Adolescents: Results from the National Comorbidity Survey Replication — Adolescent Supplement," *Journal of the American Academy of Child & Adolescent Psychiatry*, 49(10), 2010). Studies show that both conditions respond well to early treatment, particularly cognitive-behavioral therapy (Weisz, J.R., McCarty, C.A., & Valeri, S.M., "Effects of Psychotherapy for Depression in Children and Adolescents: A Meta-Analysis," *Psychological Bulletin*, 132(1), 2006). Childhood depression often presents as irritability rather than sadness (Stringaris, A., Maughan, B., Copeland, W.S., Costello, E.J., & Angold, A., "Irritable Mood as a Symptom of Depression in Youth: Prevalence, Developmental, and Clinical Correlates in the Great Smoky Mountains Study," *Journal of the American Academy of Child & Adolescent Psychiatry*, 52(8), 2013).

On self-harm in children: Research documents increasing rates of self-harm in younger age groups, with emergency room visits for self-harm in the 10-14 age group rising significantly in recent years (Mercado, M.C., Holland, K., Leemis, R.W., Stone, D.M., Wang, J., & Ivey-Stephenson, A.Z., "Trends in Emergency Department Visits for Nonfatal Self-Inflicted Injuries Among Youth Aged 10 to 24 Years in the United States, 2001-2015," *JAMA*, 318(19), 2017). Studies emphasize the importance of non-punitive response and professional intervention (Nock, M.K., "Self-Injury," *Annual Review of Clinical Psychology*,

6, 2010). Any self-harm should be taken seriously and warrants professional evaluation (Glenn, C.R. & Klonsky, E.D., "Nonsuicidal Self-Injury Disorder: An Empirical Investigation in Adolescent Psychiatric Patients," *Journal of Clinical Child & Adolescent Psychology*, 42(4), 2013).

On divorce and child outcomes: Research consistently shows that the level of parental conflict, not divorce itself, is the strongest predictor of child outcomes (Amato, P.R., "Children of Divorce in the 1990s: An Update of the Amato and Keith (1991) Meta-Analysis," *Journal of Family Psychology*, 15(3), 2001). Children whose parents maintain cooperative co-parenting relationships after divorce show outcomes similar to children from intact families (Kelly, J.B. & Emery, R.E., "Children's Adjustment Following Divorce: Risk and Resilience Perspectives," *Family Relations*, 52(4), 2003). Shielding children from interparental conflict and maintaining stable, loving relationships with both parents when possible are protective factors (Hetherington, E.M. & Kelly, J., *For Better or For Worse: Divorce Reconsidered*, W.W. Norton, 2002).

On the Tell, Show, Try, Do framework: Research supports the effectiveness of structured skill-teaching approaches that reduce cognitive load and provide safe opportunities for practice (Sweller, J., "Cognitive Load During Problem Solving: Effects on Learning," *Cognitive Science*, 12(2), 1988). Self-determination theory documents the importance of autonomy in building intrinsic motivation and ownership (Deci, E.L. & Ryan, R.M., "The 'What' and 'Why' of Goal Pursuits: Human Needs and the Self-Determination of Behavior," *Psychological Inquiry*, 11(4), 2000). Research on mastery vs. performance orientation shows that separating learning from evaluation improves outcomes and builds persistence (Dweck, C.S. & Leggett, E.L., "A Social-Cognitive Approach to Motivation and Personality," *Psychological Review*, 95(2), 1988).

On sleep in pre-adolescence: Research documents that circadian rhythms begin shifting later during this period, contributing to difficulty falling asleep at earlier bedtimes (Crowley, S.J., Acebo, C., & Carskadon, M.A., "Sleep, Circadian Rhythms, and Delayed Phase in Adolescence," *Sleep Medicine*, 8(6), 2007). Children ages 7-12 need 9-12 hours of sleep, but many get significantly less (Paruthi, S., et al., "Consensus Statement of the American Academy of Sleep Medicine on the Recommended Amount of Sleep for Healthy Children," *Journal of Clinical Sleep Medicine*, 12(6), 2016). Chronic sleep deprivation affects mood, attention, and academic performance (Dewald, J.F., Meijer, A.M., Oort, F.J., Kerkhof, G.A., & Bögels, S.M., "The Influence of Sleep Quality, Sleep Duration and Sleepiness on School Performance in Children and Adolescents: A Meta-Analytic Review," *Sleep Medicine Reviews*, 14(3), 2010).

On connection for busy parents: Research shows that quality of parent-child interaction matters more than quantity (Hsin, A. & Felfe, C., "When Does Time Matter? Maternal Employment, Children's Time With Parents, and Child Development," *Demography*, 51(5), 2014). Micro-moments of connection, protected transitions, and consistent rituals can maintain attachment even with limited time (Fiese, B.H., et al., "A Review of 50

Years of Research on Naturally Occurring Family Routines and Rituals," *Journal of Family Psychology*, 16(4), 2002). Being "fully present some of the time" is sufficient for healthy development (Milkie, M.A., Nomaguchi, K.M., & Denny, K.E., "Does the Amount of Time Mothers Spend with Children or Adolescents Matter?" *Journal of Marriage and Family*, 77(2), 2015).

About the author

David A. Smith's four-decade exploration of human patterns began long before he sold his successful business to raise his daughters. From Midwest farm beginnings through entrepreneurship and into single parenthood, he's maintained an insatiable need to understand the "why" behind everything — from how things work to where ideas originate.

Smith's studies span from ancient texts to behavioral science. The Recognition Series distills observations from single parenting, entrepreneurship, and extensive interdisciplinary study into practical insights about the invisible patterns that influence us all.

He currently lives in the United States, still asking "why?"

For more information about the Recognition Series,
visit www.recognitionpress.com

Companion Resources

This section is part of *The Foundation Years* series from Recognition Press — a research-based guide to understanding your child at every stage of development.

In this volume:

- *Before Words* (0-2) — Attachment, co-regulation, and the foundation
- *When Words Arrive* (2-5) — The word universe gap and development in action
- *The Age of Reason* (5-7) — The cognitive shift and the expanding world
- *The Forgotten Years* (7-12) — The bridge to adolescence

For deeper exploration of parent-child communication: *Why Won't You Listen? The Science of What Kids Really Hear When You Speak* by David A. Smith is the companion volume to this guide. It explores the neuroscience of parent-child communication with practical strategies, real-world examples, and techniques you can use immediately.

www.ingramcontent.com/pod-product-compliance
Ingram Content Group UK Ltd.
Pitfield, Milton Keynes, MK11 3LW, UK
UKHW021933200726
13853UKWH00010B/513

9 798999 730930